I0826915

# Prayers for Life's Journey

Owen Watson, Ph.D.

*Prayers for Life's Journey*


Author Owen Watson's books may be purchased for educational, business, or sales promotional use. For information, please email: hello@authorowenwatson.com or visit www.drowenwatson.com

First Edition

Cover Design By: Owen Watson, Ph.D.

Editor: Ramona L. Watson, Ph.D.

Library of Congress Cataloging-in-Publication Data

ISBN-9781733164139

# Dedication

This project is dedicated to those who simply seek assurance and/or reassurance that God is yet on the throne. Though at times giving up on prayer seemed to be an option, God silently spoke by presenting you a 'by-chance' opportunity of coming across this publication as affirmation of Him hearing you; He would love for the two of you to grow closer! Be strong, be encouraged, and be who He has called you to be in prayer.

# Contents

# Introduction

## Why Prayer?

It was laid upon my heart to write *Prayers for Life's Journeys* as a response to those seeking a prayer during those 'whatever' moments we commonly face in life. Those moments of 'whatever' include but are not limited to modulating expressions of loneliness, emptiness, sorrows, joys, needing guidance, forgiveness, etc. Sadly, but truthfully, for many who pray, we can and do get caught in ruts with repetitive prayers that quickly translate to praying in vain by the fact of us taking for granted prayer and the time we supposedly carve out for God.

Prayer should be a solemn time that is intentionally taken for a one-on-one conversation between you and the Creator of ALL. It is not meant to be something taken lightly or a last option. Take a second to think about the person you most admire and having an opportunity to meet that individual. In most cases, each of us will be anxious, readying ourselves by setting aside time to possibly read more about them, study their statistics or artistry, and some may even go as far as preparing a gift to bring them; most definitely, we will be ready to discuss and ask questions about them. In all of this, what we are really doing is diminishing who we are by spotlighting that individual [the person admired] in hopes of gleaning vicarious significance through a short-lived, superficial meet and greet.

If any of us can become so enamored and enthralled about a person who honestly knows nothing about us, how much more excited and ready should we be about meeting the God of the universe, who knows everything about us? Think about it – you and I have the privilege to come before GOD! He is the One who called everything into being – the galaxies, living creatures, suns and moons, all serving individual purposes that exemplify His magnificence and love.

Before taking time to pray, it is imperative that in faith we first see and recognize God as being the Source of what we are seeking. He must be realistically accepted as the "I AM" for all situations we find ourselves in, whether 'good' or 'bad'. Furthermore, it is vital that we dispel the notion of needing prayer only in times of trouble. Nothing could be less true!

Prayer is our communication with God as our Sovereign Ruler, Father, and Friend. We speak with Him candidly and without reservation, knowing that He cares, guides, comforts, provides, and answers. He is not to be viewed and/or used as a 'genie' or some sort of magical, intangible object that bows to our beck and call; neither is He someone we should fear coming before because of guilt. Plainly and simply speaking, approaching God requires: our acknowledgement by faith that He is [God] as He claimed to be; respect of Him as God; and, trusting Him with all, for all, and in all things. When our attitude is represented by these actions, we can begin to nurture our relationship with Him as we have now readied ourselves to boldly seek Him in prayer.

# Background

The question some may nervously ask, confidently believe, or timidly think, if asked to say a prayer for someone on the spot is, "Isn't there a formula for praying?" The answer is 'not necessarily' but there are some considerations we might want to be cognizant of. Although there is no one perfect formula for prayer, just like there is no one specific way you address everyone you know, there is a method that may be to our advantage as His children in faith. In other words, how we address someone is based on how we view them and/or what we are seeking from them – both require hope [faith], respect, and trust. Keep in mind, prayer is the same as you talking to a friend, co-worker, supervisor, employee, etc. – precise communication is required for proper results.

Just as we communicate with various people on different levels throughout our lives, we must make conscious efforts to adjust our position with God in how we seek Him [as He wears the hats of being a friend, co-worker, supervisor, parent, etc.]. Having a personal relationship with Him helps tremendously in recognizing the depth of His character and enhances our communications with Him personally and fine-tuned to what is specifically being presented in prayer. Each characteristic of God is depicted by either a Hebrew or Greek name which explicitly defines His position. Liken it to you knowing your mother as 'Mom', a friend of hers calling her 'Mary', an employee calling her 'Ma'am' or 'Boss', her boss calling her 'Ms.,' etc. – her title is governed by the relationship and position of authority - get the point?

*Prayers for Life's Journey* provides 50 plus names of God [in Hebrew and Greek] along with prayers to help us communicate with Him on a more personal level. Interestingly, we can find some of those names subtly being used within the Lord's prayer (Matthew 6:9-13):

| **Verse** | **Hebrew/Greek Title** | **Greek Meaning** |
| --- | --- | --- |
| Our Father | Abba[1] | Father |
| who art in heaven | Jehovah Bashayim[1] | God in Heaven |
| hallowed be your name | Elohim Kedoshim[1] | The Holy God |
| Your kingdom come | Jehovah Eli Meleki[1] | God My King |
| Thy will be done | Adonai[1] | Our Sovereign Lord/Master |
| here on earth, as it is in heaven | Jehovah Bashayim[1] | God in heaven |
| Give us this day | Jehovah-Jireh[1] | The Lord Our Provider |
| our daily bread | Lechem Ha-Chayim[1] | The Bread of life |
| and forgive us our trespasses as we forgive those who trespass against us | Jehovah El Nas[1] | The Forgiving God |
| Lead us not into temptation | Jehovah Ra'ah[1] | Lord is My Shepherd |
| but deliver us from evil | Jehovah Palat[1] | The Lord is My |

| | | Deliverer |
|---|---|---|
| For yours is the kingdom | Jehovah Sabaoth[1] | The Lord of Hosts |
| and the power | El-Gibbor[1] | Mighty God |
| and the glory | Jehovah El Hakkabod[1] | The God of Glory |
| forever | Elohim[1] | The Eternal God |

The overall intent is to assist in developing a constant prayer life as well as having a template for various prayers to use when we do not know what to pray. Know the God you serve by knowing Him beyond the title of 'God.' May the reading of this publication bless your soul and may God's favor be upon your every move according to His will and word.

# Prayers of Adoration -All About God-

# Is there really a God?

## Alēthinos Theos[1]
## "True God"

---

*And we know that the Son of God has come and has given us an understanding, that* ***we may know Him who is true****; and* ***we are in Him who is true****, in His Son Jesus Christ. This is* ***the true God*** *and eternal life.*
(1 John 5:20, NKJV)[2]

---

Just as those who do not care to know God, we as believers have oftentimes found ourselves questioning whether there's really a God, or if God is some fictitious, comforting, drummed up tool used to bring us a satisfying, ideal hope. Then again with so many conjured gods, many believers have questioned if we are serving the 'right' god. Truth be told, and even more astounding, there are ordained Christian ministers who teach others the word of God weekly from the pulpit yet battle within themselves daily the realness of His existence. Regardless of whether we are newbies or well-seasoned veterans of faith, none of us are beyond pondering any of these questionable thoughts at any particular time in our lives. What should bring us back to reality are historical facts and the witness of His love shown upon and through our lives.

Although there are many examples that can be used to justify the realness of God, I'd like for us to look at it from a personal point of view. Think about it for a minute; before having a personal relationship with God, the boundaries we lived by were governed by what satisfied and benefitted us [you and I] without many regards to how we treated others. However, that all began to change as we daily hungered and thirsted after Him as well as nurtured on His word. The closer we got to Him, the more we became like Him [in understanding and illustrating love], the less we were of our old selves, and the more we were convinced He is the true God. On the contrary, the longer we walked without Him, the less peace and sense of purpose we experienced – we had a void and an intuitive sense that something was missing. There is a measure of faith that He has given to each of us that can only be usefully satisfied when connected to Him – He's the only outlet [energy supplier] that accepts your specially designed plug [measure of faith] for correct operations. Furthermore, there is no other God that has been or is capable of loving us to the point of giving His only Son for the salvation of the world, no matter how undeserving we are, have been, or will continue to be! He yet loved us enough to conquer sin and death so that we may live because of His love and forgiveness [for we know not what we do].

Whenever you are getting to a point of questioning if He is the true God, remind yourself of the differences between the old and new you. The testimony of who you are will serve as a testimony that He is the True God. Afterward, pray with confidence in Him being "Alēthinos Theos."

## PRAYER

*Lord, Alēthinos Theos, thank You for being the unquestionable Truth above all. At times I falter in representing You in thoughts and character; however, the promised security I have being in Your hands always realigns me with truth. I pray and stand against wandering thoughts that question the integrity of who You are and the safe house of hope for which I am a part of in Christ. Let me not ever accept deceptive words from the enemy nor those who do not know or recognize You as the True God. Help me to regard You in the utmost esteem, and to walk with a godly character of integrity daily. I accept You this day and forevermore as the True God. Amen!*

# None Greater

## El Elyon[1]
## "The Most High God"

---

*Then Melchizedek king of Salem brought out bread and wine; he was the priest of* ***God Most High****.*
(Genesis 14:18, NKJV) [2]

---

Is there any other god higher than the God you know and serve? Is there any other god that has been as dependable as the God you know and serve? Is there any other god that has been a steadfast fixture positioning you as an overcomer when others have counted you out? If the answer to each of these questions is a resounding "NO", guess what? You know and serve El Elyon – The Most High God! No matter what the past holds over you, today brings against you, nor what traps are set before you, stand with confidence as a living testimony to the God Most High and humbly kneel with an attitude of gratitude and uplifted hands, offering words and songs of praise. He is God Most High and worthy of reverence well beyond what we show to those who occupy borrowed titles and positions of honor. There truly is none greater nor higher than God Most High!

Getting to a place where we individually have such a personal relationship, revelation, and appreciation of Him as being the God Most High is actually pretty simple. Consider how and why any of us are breathing life today or having made it this far. The Most High God looked on us with favor and provided a sacrifice of Himself to bridge the gap between lowly us and the God Most High. Experiences have taught us that there is no extraordinary hope to be found within ourselves nor among any other living creature. That hope can only be found when we are positioned to look beyond the natural and worship The Most High God in spirit and truth. Never cease offering praise and worship to the only deserving God!

## PRAYER

*El Elyon, I come to You humbly with uplifted hands offering gifts of praise from my lips and worship in my heart and lifestyle – may You find them acceptable. Being before You, I am in awe of the magnificence of Your presence. It's in the holy of holies where You reside, an immovable force that stabilizes the universe and my very soul with a word. As the Most High God, all is under Your authority to use and accomplish as You desire. Who shall give a false judgement to say there is no God? Let them repent and seek You for themselves that they too may fall down before You and witness Your majesty and the salvation of their souls. Regardless if we are hopeful or hopeless, help us to seek and reverence You as God Most High that our souls may be stirred in confidence and in righteousness. Lastly, I pray to be mindful of You being on the throne of eternity and for Your guidance as I live this temporal physical life to Your glory. Amen!*

# Our God

## Jehovah Eloheenu[1]
## "The Lord Our God"

---

*Exalt the* ***LORD our God****, and worship at His footstool; for He is holy. / You answered them, O* ***LORD our God;*** *You were to them God-Who-Forgives, though You took vengeance on their deeds. / Exalt the* ***LORD our God****, and worship at His holy hill; for the* ***LORD our God*** *is holy.*
(Psalms 99:5, 8, 9, NKJV)[2]

---

Living life as a believer, at times we stumble in our self-righteous judgement of others partly due to being accustomed to seeing Him personally and solely as "my God." While it is imperative for each of us to have a personal relationship with Him as "my God," it would crucially behoove us to see others through Him. In doing so, we catch the revelation that He is Jehovah Eloheenu (The Lord our God). Seeing Him as such allows us to exact the same grace and mercy on others as He has on us. That revelation enhances our ability to withhold judgment and release prayer and assistance instead. Possessing Him as "The Lord our God" positions each of us as a family member, with each bringing their own testimony, talent, and/or gift that supports the extending of His kingdom here on earth as it is in heaven. The next time any of us observes a fellow believer going off course, let us first see Him as Jehovah Eloheenu then reserve judgment and pull alongside to pray and/or offer appropriate assistance to them as God has done and continues to do for us through others.

## PRAYER

*Holy and Righteous You are, Jehovah Eloheenu. I offer praises unto You with my awakening breath until my time of resting for the evening. There is none like You nor comparable to You. You are so much more than we could ever describe in words. Your love is immeasurable, and Your knowledge and wisdom are endless. To say there is no God, is to be the walking dead, for all that exists is by Your hand and for serving a purpose for all Who call upon Your name. Thanks for Your pure and unconditional love. Thanks for equipping us with various abilities and guiding us safely through life's journey. Thanks for being longsuffering. Thanks for Your peace. Thanks for Your hearing and attentiveness. Thanks for Your grace and mercy. Thanks for Your favor upon the lesser among us to do great things. Thanks for helping us to see and become useful for the bigger picture of purpose. Thanks for Your healings and deliverances. Thanks for the timeout periods You have established that we may connect or reconnect with You. Thanks for Your unspeakable joy. Thanks for being forgiving and enabling us to do likewise. Thanks for instilling within us courage and comfort by your Holy Spirit. Thank you for how, when, and where we each were born and developing each of our testimonies unto Your glory. I raise a hallelujah to You, "The Lord Our God," this day and forevermore! Amen.*

# Blessed Assurance

## El-Olam[1]
## "The Everlasting God"

*And Abraham planted a grove in Beersheba, and called there on the name of the* ***LORD****, the* ***Everlasting God****.*
(Genesis 21:33, KJV)[2]

Though there are countless views of how we each see God, there is one that really stands out as most prominent to me. And that is seeing Him as El-Olam (The Everlasting God). Being El-Olam brings a sense of security in knowing there is no end in sight for His presence and faithfulness in our lives. It signifies His undying love, strength, peace, and protection. In times where we suffer loss of saved loved ones, we are assured of them living on in a place of peace with Him; likewise, He comforts and strengthens us beyond our loss and becomes our testimony of peace to share with others. When we grow weary and weak, He reignites within us the will and strength required to press forward.

As El-Olam, there is no giving up, wearing down, or shortage of His faithfulness. He brings hope beyond death and despair. He is our watchman and protector in moments of darkness that we experience. He is our escape when we are backed into a corner and have given and/or taken all we could give or take. He is our everlasting source for all of our needs. He is El-Olam! Never doubt where He is; just keep doing, praying, giving, and trusting because He is there to take up the slack, pull us forward, and wrap us in His glory as His children.

## PRAYER

*Lord, El-Olam, how joyous and reassuring it is to know that You are here which keeps hopes and promises alive: hopes in us overcoming obstacles and promises for us getting through them as well as hopes and promises of us attaining brighter futures. In the faces of fear, doubt, and death, You will see to the destruction of such by empowering and calling us to rise above them all as we extend our hand to Yours. It is in Your hands that we are forever secured and comforted not only here on earth but even in the afterlife. I pray for You to help us not lose faith and to trust You as the God of tomorrow just as You have proven to be during past times. Today is what is, but time cannot contain El-Olam; therefore, bless us with a promising hope of victory in the tomorrow before us. Amen!*

# Set Apart

## Elohim Kedoshim[1]
## "The Holy God"

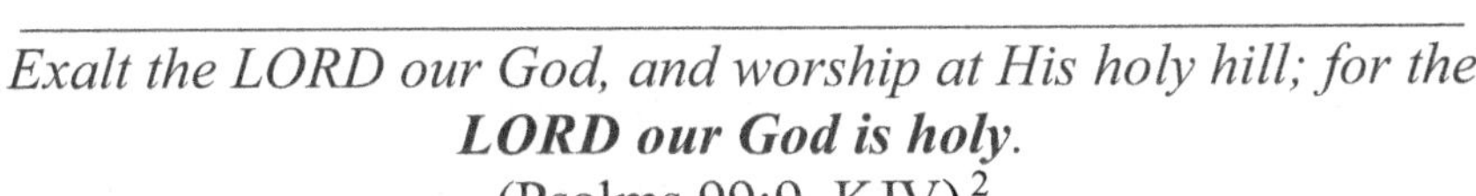

*Exalt the LORD our God, and worship at His holy hill; for the* ***LORD our God is holy****.*
(Psalms 99:9, KJV)[2]

God is not a figment of our imagination. He is not some genie who helplessly grants our every wish and desire. He is not a created human being, driven by selfish emotionalism. He is not our equal, whom we can disrespect, disregard, or control. He is not somewhere in hiding awaiting an opportunity to show up on the scene. He is not a carved image made by human hands. He is not an animal. He is not an astrological god.

He is Elohim Kedoshim – "The Holy God." He is set apart based on Who He is and only can be – the Supreme Being of time, space, and all creation! He does not cast a shadow, operate within time as we know it, nor contain any weakness or flaws about Him. When He speaks, life itself, in various forms, breaks forth in existence and is stationed according to His will. His very thoughts cause creation to respond – look at the sun shining, observe the formation of the stars, and witness your ability to breathe what you cannot see.

Let us reverence, praise, and worship Him, not as we do mankind, particular dates or events of significance, but as Elohim Kedoshim. He is the omniscient, omnipotent, and omnipresent originator and ruler of all that has ever existed. Who are we, created by Him, to lessen His holiness?

## PRAYER

*Elohim Kedoshim – none before, none after, none other that exists. I praise and worship You who are set apart and maintain order according to Your will and plan for what is best for all. Your nature proves Your essence of being awesome, loving, powerful, kind, caring, and so much more! As I come before You, I pray that all mankind thoughtfully considers and acknowledges, in heart, mind, and spirit, Your holiness with utmost respect. Awaken those of us who discount Your existence, look to and trust in false gods, or insincerely come before You with vain prayers, praise, and worship. I ask Your forgiveness and an opening of hearts, minds, and spirits to receive spiritual and natural sight to witness the evidence of Your holiness.*

*In seeing, may we know our place and look up to You as Elohim Kedoshim. Amen!*

# Be Grateful

## Jah[1]
## "God That Rides Upon The Heavens"

---

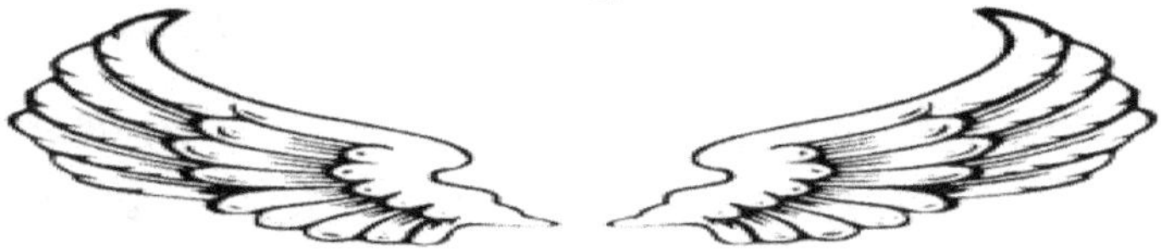

*Sing unto God, sing praises to His name: extol Him that rideth upon the heavens by His name **JAH**, and rejoice before Him.*
(Psalms 68:4, KJV)[2]

---

There have been and will continue to be times when we do not know what to pray about or for; it is common among all of us as believers. When times like those arise, it presents an opportunity for us to bask in His glory. It is an opportunity for us to magnify Him as Jah (God that rides upon the heavens) – knowing that He is ever watching over us, protecting us, and guiding the winds and changing the course of our lives for the good. As we look to Him, the clouds and sky themselves magnify His presence – let us recognize and follow suit. He shadows us from the fiery sun rays and provides rain for our thirsty souls in times of famine. He sees and stands ready to intervene throughout our life journeys. He is Jah!

## PRAYER

*Father, I come before you empty of words but thankful of your presence as Jah. Thankful I am, for this day. A day when silence rules my thoughts and lips unless I speak to you in vain. Not knowing what lies ahead, I know that You are there to provide needed peace and protection. I submit my mind of worries to You to carry far away with the winds. I stand willing and ready to receive Your outpouring for the nurturing of my mind and comfort of my soul. You are the awesome and magnificent God that we look too. You are the great and mighty God who protects us. You are the loving and comforting God we need. You are the God who starts and finishes the race with us. Though my words be few, I shall rest my cares upon the greatness of who You are – Jah! Grant me strength to worship you in word and deed, always remembering that I am Your child and Your goodness and mercy follows after me. I love and bless You this day. Amen.*

# It's Not Over

## Jehovah El-Emunah[1]
## "The Faithful God"

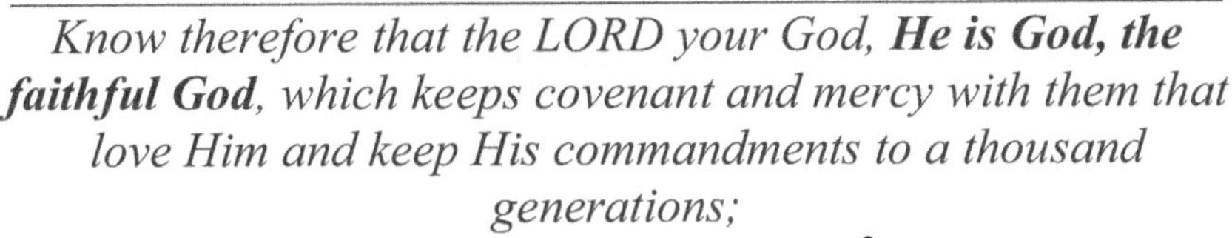

---

*Know therefore that the LORD your God, **He is God, the faithful God**, which keeps covenant and mercy with them that love Him and keep His commandments to a thousand generations;*
(Deuteronomy 7:9, KJV)[2]

---

At some point in life, we all have or will experience disruptions that shake our foundation of faith and shatter our hopes and plans. Whether it be divorce, loss of employment, income disruption, bad life decisions, etc., as devastating either of those circumstance may be, as long as there's Jehovah El-Emunah, it's not over. As His children, we share in the promise of His faithfulness to those who love Him and follow after Him.

Surely, we will grieve – it is a right of expression and emotional outlet He created within us. It's okay to mourn for whatever has been lost. However, I implore you not to lose faith in the process because good news awaits – He is faithfully with us and ready to pull each of us from the ashes.

We serve a faithful God Who honors covenant – He will never leave nor forsake us and He takes care of what belongs to Him. Rest assured that God is incapable of failing and because He is love as well, He will faithfully comfort us by stabilizing the raging storms and winds that come upon us. Those storms and winds may strip away our cares, but they have no effect on the immovable God we serve. As one tornado causes a loss and much damage, the faithfulness of God comes behind like a hurricane pouring into our lives not only what is needed but replacing the losses with blessings far above what was ever expected. Do not lose heart, hope, or peace – He is Jehovah El-Emunah, our evidence that it is not over.

## PRAYER

*Lord, faithful are You far more than we could ever endure. Where there is testing, You are revealed as the Answer. Where there is loss, You are revealed as the Restorer. Where there is mourning, You are revealed as our Joy. Where there is hopelessness, You are revealed as evidence of hope. Where there is fear, You are revealed as Courage. Where there are storms and violent winds, You are revealed as Peace. Thank You for Your faithfulness even during times of my faithlessness. I am revived by the knowledge and wisdom of seeing You as Jehovah El-Emunah. I praise You this day and everyday, not only for what comes my way, but whatever comes Your children's way collectively. We praise You and pray to be reminded of connecting our faithlessness to the charge station of Jehovah El-Emunah for a recharge of surety that it's not over. Bless Your Holy name, I pray. Amen.*

# Mistakes Made

## Jehovah Shaphat[1]
## "The Lord is Our Judge"

*For the **LORD is our judge**, the LORD is our lawgiver, the LORD is our king; he will save us.*
(Isaiah 33:22, KJV)[2]

Every mistake we have ever made came with a judge. The judge can be us personally, a magistrate, victims of our mistakes, or spectators. Mistakes never go unnoticed and are always measured against what is thought of as correct or right. We all make mistakes in life. Some of those mistakes were excused and some cost us dearly as they continued to follow us through life. The mistakes we make in life not only prove we are fallible, but they come with judgment. Being the judge of our own mistakes, we can and oftentimes do excuse them; but in the eyes of someone else who judges, there is often a price to be paid.

Before committing our lives to God, we did everything within our power to cover mistakes in life. We would even go as far as believing that false slogan of 'only God can judge me.' Whether we like it or not, others possess a right to judge whomever. If not, then we must do away with standards of what is true or false, right or wrong, and acceptable or not acceptable. Truthfully, we are all deserving of inescapable righteous judgment whether we are God's children or not. As a matter of fact, in 1 Corinthians 5:12-13, Paul speaks about God judging those on the outside, and we who are in the family of Christ are to judge one another. We must understand that judging is basically inspecting the evidence when there is questionable, unbecoming conduct.

As believers, we represent and serve under Jehovah Shaphat. He is the Righteous Judge Who not only reviewed the evidence against us, but dismissed the charges after the penalty price was paid by His Son. In doing so, we have an obligation as His children to learn from the past life we lived, honor the price that was paid, and please Him in living life going forward. God is not to be mocked and we are not to be stumbling blocks for others He is using us to reach. Respecting the law of His word written upon our hearts helps us to live a virtuous life because the Lord is our Judge.

## PRAYER

*Lord, You alone are the Righteous Judge above all. It is before You that we shall all stand to be judged whether in this life or the life to come. Help our hearts to be sensitively aware of Who we are representing at all times. Keep us from reverting to old habits which dismiss Your presence and welcome darkness. May we live honorable and respectable lives that distance us far from shame. Even as Your children, we all continue to make mistakes daily. But because of the acceptance of Christ in our lives and You as Judge, You wash us clean as we bring those matters before You. Thanks for Your everlasting and enduring mercies and kindness You provide us with daily. Fill us with integrity and renew us with refined character as we give our lives to You. Help us to be accountable to one another for the good and in love without any inkling of having a 'holier-than-thou' attitude. Long live Jehovah Shaphat! Amen.*

# Prayers for Strength

# Power

## El-Gibbor[1]
## "The Mighty God"

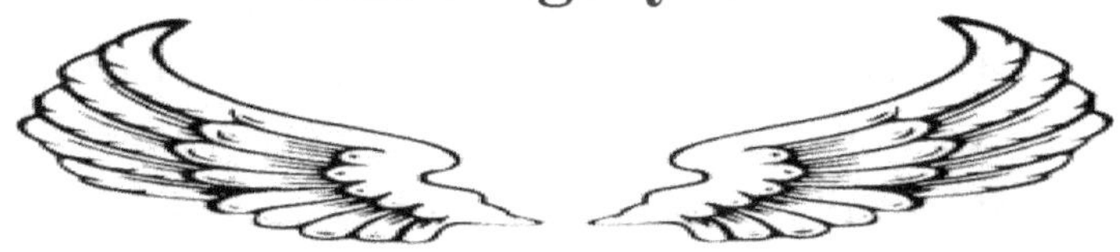

---

*For unto us a Child is born, unto us a Son is given; and the government will be upon His shoulder. And His name shall be called Wonderful, Counsellor,* ***Mighty God****, Everlasting Father, Prince of Peace.*
(Isaiah 9:6, NKJV)[2]

---

At some point in time, some if not all of us have experienced being short-tempered whereas we allowed negative and condescending words people said to or about us to trigger a non-Christian response that we may [or may not] have regretted later. Nevertheless, there was seemingly always some sort of discipline following our actions, whether it was inner spiritual conviction, physical harm, broken relationships, job loss, or tangible legal consequences. Whatever the form of discipline we received, it all served a learning purpose of maintaining self-control. In our own power it is nearly impossible to achieve, especially when someone catches us on a not-so-good day. Sadly, it results in too many of us being on a merry-go-around where we repeatedly give the same response and suffer the same or more drastic consequences.

As believers, we ultimately grieve the spirit of God within by rejecting His wisdom and power. What God counts as a win in our favor is not by actions of defense that sway us out of character as His children. God's win comes on our behalf when we see and experience Him as El-Gibbor, "The Mighty God", by way of His spirit within us. His spirit simply guides us with the power of maintaining our peace, peace with others, and surrendering the 'case' to Him in prayer to defend on our behalf. I challenge you to get off the merry-go-around and discover what new ground God has for you as you rely on Him as El-Gibbor.

## PRAYER

*El-Gibbor, The Mighty God, there is nothing you cannot handle, nothing that is able to overtake you – You are Power, You are Strong, and You are with us and within us. Thank You for opening my ears to hear You speak the words "I got this" and the eyes of my heart to see You at work within me. No longer do I wish to – nor will I – appease this flesh and behave in a manner contradictory to Your word. You are the Mighty God that accomplishes by Your Spirit. It is that same spirit that enabled Christ to endure much, even to the point of death; and, that same spirit that proclaimed victory at His rising. That is the exact Spirit of power You have given Your children that we too may overcome by focusing on the mission at hand, not the offenses coming by many hands. In those moments when I am tempted and apt to give someone a piece of my mind, let it be the mind of Christ rather than of flesh. Help me to defer to You when troubles arise so that I may not fight in my own strength but by the Spirit of The Mighty God leading within. Amen!*

# Help is Beside You

## Elohim Azar[1]
## "God Our Helper"

---

*Behold,* ***God is my helper****; the Lord is with those who uphold my life.*
(Psalms 54:4, NKJV)[2]

---

Upon discharge from the U.S. Navy in 1998, I'd obtained employment with the postal service in northeast Arkansas. In the year 2000, while selected to be a supervisor, I encountered much resistance from the employees I was in charge of leading. The troubles ranged from false accusations to numerous grievances for any and everything to intentionally slowing down the processing of mail. As those atrocious acts were going on, I remember how I would daily, while at work and driving to and from work, doing just as Jesus instructed His disciples in

Matthew 5:44, "…Love your enemies, bless them that curse you, do good to them that hate you, and pray for them which despitefully use you, and persecute you." I followed those instructions to heart although many times I was questioning God and trying to figure out what I was doing so wrong for them to behave how they were.

Out of the blue, one day one of the workers [Dan] approached and pulled me aside and explained the reasoning behind the resistance. He stated it was due to the facts of me being a Yankee (because of being originally from Chicago), being an African American in charge of a large group of Caucasians in the south, and being a military veteran – meaning veterans received hiring preference which many of the civilian workers viewed as cutting job opportunities for those having no military affiliation. That very same day, another worker [Jimmy] approached me and stated that he would start being my lookout; he began by showing me places some of the employees were misplacing trays of mail for later deliveries rather than grouping them with their regular deliveries. This was intentionally done for a reason to have me removed as supervisor if discovered by the Postmaster upon receiving complaints from the contracted customers. Thanks to Dan, I was at peace after gaining an understanding of the employees' gripes. And thanks to Jimmy, I was given a heads-up on the misplaced mail so that I was able to catch it at every turn and get all the mail out as prescribed.

Reflecting on this story, I clearly see the hand of Elohim Azar (God My Helper) at work. The help God provided through Dan and Jimmy benefitted my life greatly during those times of needed peace, understanding, and good work performance. Ironically, within a year, they both attained managerial positions.

Whether partly because of them being used to intervene in my life had something to do with it, I cannot say for certain, but I strongly believe that by the grace of Elohim Azar, He granted favor in their lives.

We cannot afford to walk blindly and discard everyone as being against us, while constantly praying to God for help. As we pray and seek Elohim Azar, be prepared for His answer, sometimes through the most unlikely people around us.

## PRAYER

*Elohim Azar, in times of need You alone establish the parameters of hurts, harms, and dangers that come against us; and You alone bestow favor and grace in our lives for overcoming each. Help us in not allowing weariness and worries to cloud our vision of Your help among us. Help us to remain faithful and diligent in praying, loving, doing good, and blessing others by the power of Your Spirit within us and as evidence of being Your ambassadors. Let us not lose heart in purpose nor lose sight of knowing You are our present help in times of need. As we receive Your help from whomever You choose to send as our aid, may an extension of Your favor be granted in their lives accordingly. You are Lord, You are our Helper. Amen!*

# Look Before Blaming

## Elohim Qarob[1]
## "God is Near"

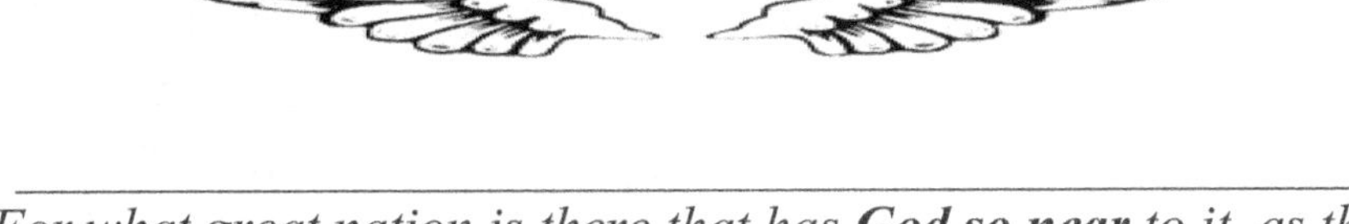

---

*For what great nation is there that has* ***God so near*** *to it, as the LORD our* ***God is to us****, for whatever reason we may call upon Him?*
(Deuteronomy 4:7, NKJV)[2]

---

Live long enough and you too will join the club of feeling deserted as most of us aged folks have. The roughest patch is when no one is able to bring you comfort and peace, not even the person you consider closest to you. There was one point in life when I was really going through a turbulent situation. I would reach out to find solace among those closest to me. The conversations and advice provided were comforting for the moment but very soon after I would find myself back in a rut within my thoughts and dealing with anxiety. To make matters worse, I was nowhere physically located near those particular folks where either they or I could have traveled within minutes for a physical presence of comfort. All conversations took place over the phone. Calling and talking was better than no communication at all and I have always appreciated the times we talked. However, after the phone calls, I was still in a state of feeling deserted, not so much by the support group I had, but by God.

I would spend numerous hours and days in prayer questioning God's presence. Blaming Him for my sorrows because of Him not being present to stop the hurt and pain I was experiencing. This went on for about 30 days or so. Then one day as I was preparing to go to the office, I heard this voice so audibly in my spirit, asking, "Are you ready to move forward?" The only words I could utter were 'YES, LORD." Suddenly, I experienced flashbacks of God being nearer than what I credited Him as being. He was near and manifested in the support group I had, He was near during my living day after day, He was near when I was asleep, He was near when I felt hopeless and helpless, and He was near in my prayers and hope. I was blinded so much by my trials that I failed to recognize He was near. It is so good to know that He is still near!

Let's not allow trials, people, nor things blind our sight of God's nearness. He loves us too much to ever leave us. He is Elohim Qarob!

## PRAYER

*Lord, I acknowledge Elohim Qarob this very moment! No matter my position in life, You are near for whatever reason I may have to call upon You. I pray against being consumed by what I see in the natural – making whatever it may be bigger than You. You are near to hear, deliver, provide, and so much more! All others may fail but You are near at all times. In the hurts, pains, sufferings, valleys, fires, highs and lows of life, etc. You are near protecting us and waiting to answer our prayers of faith. Renew our minds in the reality of Your nearness and may our spirits serve as witnesses in the fullness of Your presence. May we worship You by drawing nearer to You and no longer worship our problems by magnifying them. As sure as You are the Way, You are near for us to follow. Help us Lord, I pray. Amen.*

# Breaking Free

## Ha'Poretz[1]
## "The Breaker"

***The One who breaks open*** *will come up before them; they will break out, pass through the gate, and go out by it; their king will pass before them, with the LORD at their head.*
(Micah 2:13, NKJV)[2]

Living in a time where exhibitions of hate are so blatantly common throughout society and seemingly outpacing love, the entire world could use a breakthrough of Jesus now more than ever before. People hate religions, sex orientations, races, looks, etc.; some people even hate being loved. It is unfortunate how someone chooses to dedicate so much time to hating, which benefits no one, including themselves. Maybe a bit extreme but this is merely an example of how anyone is susceptible to being stuck in something that others consider senseless. We are all vulnerable. Whether it be laziness, addictions, prejudices, greed, etc. we all have a vice that imprisons and immobilizes our forward movement in certain areas of our lives.

The way out of being stuck is latching on to someone who is able to help pull us out. As our King, Jesus is most certainly qualified to do just that. As a matter of fact, He has already proven His power by breaking us free from the power of sin as we trust and follow Him. In that loving and powerful breakthrough also came the equipping and opportunity for each of us to do the same with any strongholds in our lives. We must remember and follow the lead of Ha'Poretz, Jesus the Christ.

## PRAYER – "Addictions"

*Lord, Ha'Poretz, I need your help. Help in breaking the chains of addictions. Addictions that are designed to bring harm and a dissolving of who and Whose we are. Addictions that abandon the love and care that others extend toward us as well as halt the love and care we desire to give. Lord, of my own will and power, I am totally incapable of breaking free from what I willfully choose to cling to and have given power over me. My addiction has hindered my relationship with family and friends, it has cost me employment opportunities and promotions, and it has distorted my view of love. I cannot go any further nor do I have any other option for deliverance besides You. I apologize for discarding You, your word, your sacrifice, and Your realm of protection. I ask Your forgiveness. I ask for You to take the lead in restoring me as Your child. I give myself to You for doing what must be done, that I may humbly follow after You, broken in Your hands and rebuilt for Your will. Lord, let not another day pass that I remain in the enemy's camp – even when the enemy is my very own mind. Let not another day pass that I squander purpose. Let not another day pass where I lose track of You. I pray for You to be my focus, Your love to be my addiction, and Your Spirit to be my guide. I see my need for You and would like to represent You in spirit and truth like never before. Have mercy on me, Lord, and grant me this breakthrough, I pray. Amen.*

## PRAYER – "Hereditary Habits"

*God, I seek You for a breaking of bad habits. Repeating habits that produce no growth have become the norm for me. Some have caused complacency, some have cost me relationships, and some have made me super-driven to work; but, all have produced a malnourished spiritual life. Sure, I have proclaimed Your name when something exciting has happened and cried out to You when the not-so-good has happened. It was like a classified relationship where I only communicated with You on a need-to-know basis. That too was a vain habit. Lord, I shamefully come before You with this unfruitful mess that I have created. Nothing of it has been beneficial to the relationship between You and I. As I pray this prayer, I hear You speaking words of life, that 'all things work together for my good' if I humble myself to truly seek You. I am humbly coming before You, seeking You, and desiring You to intervene for a breakthrough in the bad choices and habits I have made – including habits that hinder me from seeking You, knowing You, and loving You. Of my own strength, I cannot change a thing about these habits. But, I know by the power of Your spirit and my believing and trusting You, those bad habits can be dismissed as new genuine, godly habits are developed. I pray for Your hearing, forgiving, and breaking this child of Yours free for a more personal and meaningful relationship with You. Time is not a factor when the present is all I have. In this moment, I want to rekindle our relationship on a deeper level. I know You love me, help me to show love in return and exemplify love and light in this world as Ha'Poretz leads. Amen.*

## PRAYER – "Laziness"

*Lord, I welcome You as the Breaker from where I am. Time seems to have subtly passed by while I have been planted in a state of laziness. No fruit is there to show of positively impacting anyone's life and most of all, I have been MIA (missing in action) from representing You. Sadly, even the opportunities of catching Your word on television or radio, I have frequently tuned out just to satisfy a passion of laziness. Lord, I apologize and ask Your forgiveness. Though many actions in my life have been worthless thus far, I am asking and praying for You to help me defeat the spirit of laziness that has been prevalent over me and to renew within me a righteous and effective spirit and mind unto your glory. I realize I have been on the sidelines and out of the game far too long – that is not where You would have me to be. I am surrendering and yielding to You the right to position and use me accordingly. In Your word it is proclaimed that "the harvest is plenty, but the laborers are few." Help me in being a laborer, sharing Your love in word and in deed by faith. I'm ready to get in the game as Your hands and feet, working toward the betterment of others as a testimony of Your greatness. Prevent me from being the missing link in someone else's purpose and/or life (any longer). I pray for You to uplift, energize, and help me to focus on walking out and completing the task at hand by the power of Your Holy Spirit. I need You, I surrender to You, I invite You to take charge of this borrowed life. Glory unto You for what is ahead in my journey as I am moved from laziness to a workman diligently sharing the good news – however, wherever, whenever, and to whoever. Thanks for hearing my plea, accepting my heart's desire, and providing the necessary*

*tool (your Spirit) to carve out my dedicated testimony to You, Ha'Poretz. Amen.*

## PRAYER – "Life cycle of being Stuck / Going in circles trying to get ahead"

*Lord, I invite You into my life as Ha'Poretz. At every turn as I strive to get ahead, there is a setback. Whether it be my emotions, fears, or the past, the hurdles seem endless and always apparent just when I think I am on track for entering a better level of living. Lord, I come to You for understanding and direction for getting unstuck. I know there are lessons to be learned through experiences as well as consequences resulting from choices we have made along the way. However, it appears I have been going around this mountain far too long and it always leads me back to crying out to You. I am at a loss for understanding how to break free from this life-consuming circle. Lord, I pray for an open heart and eyes to receive your reasoning for these setbacks so that I may turn from my ways and walk in Your way. Whether it is impatience, anger, anxiety, etc. on my part, I lay it all at Your feet that I may learn and move forward in Your ways and by Your Spirit. Open my eyes to the wrong that I must address. Open my heart towards genuinely worshipping You by the way I treat others. Lord, please deal with me, Your child, with compassion and gentleness. Set my sights upon You and Your word, the Light, that I may not reflect humanity's responses of darkness – operating out of the flesh. Break my will and my mind free of selfishness and seeking appreciation from others rather than accepting the love of Your sacrifice for my life. Lord, I am desperate for becoming unstuck and request Your healing in this moment of brokenness. I desire to truly worship You. I am going to worship You with a made-up mind to bless You at all times. Lord, have Your way in the breaking and be glorified in leading my life according to Your will. I receive of You all that I need to break free. I bless You. I thank You. Amen.*

# Trouble No More

## Jehovah El Achba[1]
## "God That Hides"

---

*For in the time of trouble* ***He shall hide me*** *in his pavilion: in the secret of His tabernacle shall* ***He hide me****; He shall set me up upon a rock. /* ***You are my hiding place****; You shall preserve me from trouble; You shall compass me about with songs of deliverance.*

(Psalms 27:5 / 32:7, KJV)[2]

---

Have you ever experienced a time of being surrounded by calamity that affected others but did not shake or touch you at all? We see moments like company layoffs, sicknesses, and even people gossiping untruthful and bad things about us as storms designed to take us out. This is not to say whether or not everyone is deserving of those devastating situations, but it is to make known that we as God's children are not exempt from them. Scripturally, we all know that He rains upon the just as well as the unjust. The difference comes when He provides His children a hiding place through the form of an "umbrella" of peace, comfort, and joy to help get us through the storms unscathed. This is no more than God's favor.

He positions us in a hiding place that requires faith and trust to access. Sadly, some of us as believers refuse to be hidden and rather weather the storm the same as everyone else – either because we do not know of His hiding place, are too prideful to accept His hiding place, or have become too comfortable fighting in our own strength – resulting in mental and physical anguish. We often hear the cliché "favor isn't fair"; nothing can be further from the truth! In actuality, favor is fair when you are in the grace of the one who is providing favor. It is that person's choice to provide favor at their discretion – it is in their possession to keep or exercise! For us as believers, it should be a lifestyle of faith that keeps God's favor upon our lives, hiding and protecting us from troubles of the world. One great note about God hiding us is that He makes it no secret, He does it in plain sight much to the ignorance of others and as a testimony to us knowing Him as Jehovah El Achba.

## PRAYER

*Jehovah El Achba, my hiding place. I thank You for Your protection against the storms of life and winds of destruction. Your favor is our testimony to those around. When others are troubled with worries and losses, You faithfully hide us in plain sight with a covering that blocks destruction's attempts of coming our way. Although we compassionately continue steadfast in prayer for others, we are shielded from experiencing the surrounding devastation. May our souls be convicted to shout a praise of Thanks to You! You've provided by becoming the sacrificial offering required for our hope and faith. Under that same shed blood, You protect and wash us clean. Touch the eyes of our hearts to recognize our hiding place in You, that neither fears nor temptations blind us from Your daily favor. Lord, I shall always unashamedly bless You in songs of praise and worship! Amen.*

# You Are Good to Go

## Jehovah Maginnenu[1]
## "The Lord Our Defense"

---

*For* ***the LORD is our defense****; and the Holy One of Israel is our king.*
(Psalms 89:18, KJV)[2]

---

All too often we give more weight to the fear of what is said about us or done to us by others than we do our faith in God. Carrying that weight of fear heavily affects our vision and distorts our judgment. As their words and/or actions become all we see and talk fearfully about, we begin worrying about further harm they may bring upon us and trying our best to appease the source(s). It even affects our relationship with God as we either pray less to Him or beg for Him to protect us from the 'wrath of mankind.' In essence, those whom we fear become our god as we exalt the supposed power they have. The more they say and do against us, the more we spread the news of their actions, which only instills fear in others as a contagious disease does. Just as the enemy of God would like to see, we become fainthearted, faithless believers, easily and powerlessly tossed about.

As believers, our relationship with the God of all should be one where we can open our eyes and see Him as we need Him. If not, we will soon become comfortable living defeated lives. In the instance above, our eyes would need to see Jehovah Maginnenu – The Lord our Defense. He is our protection against all that comes against us. We are not rebuilt by Him to cower down but to stand up in the face of fear. Standing up in this case is simply presenting and relying on the word of God rather than what is said or done by others against us. They want to fire you without cause; the Lord is Your Defense – You are protected, they cannot touch you. They want to defame your character; the Lord is Your Defense – people know the truth of your character. They want to set traps for you; the Lord is Your Defense – He transforms and uses those same traps against them. Stop the worrying and being fearful – meditate on and know, JEHOVAH MAGINNENU!!!

## PRAYER

*Jehovah Maginnenu, You are our impenetrable protection! As we walk with and are wrapped in You, there is no harm that can touch us. I pray for a sealed mind containing Your word, a heart that lives Your word, and an ear that hears Your word to keep me from temptations of fear. Let my soul be at rest in Your peace, that my faith may refrain from being shaken or stirred about in favor of the enemy. As You protect us, the victory is before us for the battle is Yours. You are worthy of continual praise and worship and I shall gladly do so. You are the Lord our Defense an unbreachable force that protects and in Whom all needs are met. With You as our Defense, we are good to go as You lead. Help us to stand encouraged daily and to walk in confidence. I thank you, Lord, evermore. Amen.*

# Unbearable for a Moment

## Jehovah Ma'Ozi[1]
## "The Lord Our Strength"

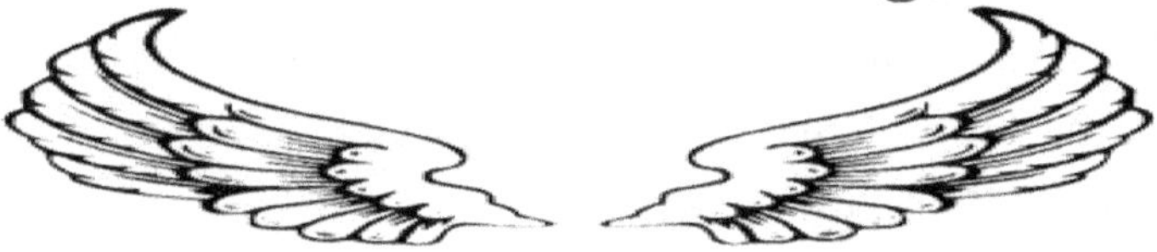

---

***The LORD is my strength*** *and song, and He is become my salvation: He is my God, and I will prepare Him an habitation; my father's God, and I will exalt Him.*
(Exodus 15:2, KJV)[2]

---

During difficult situations such as job loss, aging, divorces, failures, injuries, etc., we often turn to sorrowful 'woe is me' type songs to help bring relief. All they seem to bring are memories of how it was when things were good, what happened that made things go downhill, and negative expectations of what tomorrow may bring. Without question, the hurt and pain in our hearts are very real and needs to be dealt with. However, it is important how we choose to deal with them. What transpired weakens our emotional stability and makes us vulnerable and susceptible to not-so-good quick fixes. When we are driven to alcohol, drugs, or sorrowful 'woe is me' songs, those things only fuel those negative emotions we are wrestling with, oftentimes resulting in some individuals taking negative actions against the source they blame for causing the hurt and pain.

The great thing about God is that He is the answer for all that comes our way. In this scenario of experiencing difficult situations, we need to recognize Him as Jehovah Ma'Ozi – The Lord our Strength. We cannot see this by turning to drugs, alcohol, and sorrowful music. Those things only block the view of us seeing Him clearly. As believers, and having a lifestyle of faith, it would be to our advantage to always have a song in heart that positions us in the presence of Jehovah Ma'Ozi to settle our souls with peace that only He can provide. He is a strong God Who is more than capable of handling our unbearable situations. It is true that no one can put a timeframe on the hurt and pain anyone incurs, but there is a bigger truth knowing, as believers, that we have a God who is standing by to help us bear the load. Jehovah Ma'Ozi is not only on the throne above all the heavens, but His spirit is also the empowering source within us.

## PRAYER

*Lord, You are my strong God – how easily I forget. Thanks for awakening and reigniting my hope in You for comfort. I had my moments of mishandling my hurt and pain. I now surrender them into Your hands. I pray for revelation and acceptance of You as my strength. I pray to be made better through this grieving process and stronger for serving You in the future You have set before me. Lord, please remove any and all inclinations of me reaching to unfruitful sources in search of what only You can provide – true and sustaining peace and comfort. I ask that You place a song within to strengthen me and help me remember that You are with me. I bless You as I rely on You as Jehovah Ma'Ozi. Amen.*

# Sing Your Song

## Jehovah Palat[1]
## "The Lord is My Deliverer"

---

***You are my hiding place;* You** *shall* **preserve me** *from trouble;*
**You** *shall* **compass me** *about* **with songs of deliverance.**
(Psalms 32:7, KJV)[2]

---

There will be times beyond our past when we are doing what is right before God and others, and we will still find ourselves in the dungeon based on false accusations. There is a scripture in the Bible (Philippians 4:11-13) that talks about having learned to be content in all things. Being content in all things is not selective based on when things are going 'good' or seeing vengeance taken upon your accusers. Being content in all things means exactly as it states – ALL THINGS. The significance of being content in all things is how it causes us to rely heavily upon God, thereby strengthening our faith. When doing what is right costs us our jobs, relationships, etc., it is not to say that God does not care or is punishing us. God allows these type situations to occur for multiple reasons. Three reasons that I have witnessed in my life as well as observed in the lives of others I know personally are 1) to protect us, 2) to develop us, and 3) to promote us.

When our eyes are open in relationship with God to see behind the scenes and know He is allowing what is being done, we can be content, and rest assured with a song proclaiming Him as Jehovah Palat. Just to be clear, that song can only come about when we become content in our faith walk, not the struggle. Having that song to sing is key to our deliverance. There is no need for Him to come to our rescue when we are catering to worry. Instead, He enters in the midst of us praising Him in song. Whether we are in prison, a lion's den or a fiery furnace, God has a way of touching the heart of the very one who put you there, that they not only release you, but compensate you with favor. Know Him, know Jehovah Palat!

## PRAYER

*Jehovah Palat, thanks for setting the conditions for developing me to glorify You. Oftentimes I have wondered what I was doing so wrong to have such tragedies enter my life. I thought I was left for the enemy to destroy at will. My faith was challenged, Your existence was in question, and my dreams were shattered. Then Your spirit quieted me within that I may reflect on Your faithfulness in times past. As I pondered, I began to rejoice. I knew without a doubt You were yet on the throne. I began singing a song about You being the Almighty Jehovah Palat. You set the boundaries of our imprisoned time with a purpose. You deliver when we are developed and promote when we are ready. As a testimony, You shut the mouths of those fighting against us. Whereas they would love to curse us, they can do nothing less than bless us. Lord, I give You praise and honor as the Deliverer of my soul and physical being. Contentment is my friend, and a song in Your peace is my offering of praise to You. Thank You, Lord and be glorified! Amen.*

# Looking Ahead by Memories

## Jehovah Roi[1]
## "The God Who Sees"

---

*Then she called the name of the LORD who spoke to her,* ***You-are-the-God-Who-Sees;*** *for she said, "Have I also here seen Him who sees me?"*
(Genesis 16:13, NKJV)[2]

---

For us not to return where we come from, we must look ahead. Sounds easy but many can attest that it can be very difficult to do, especially after losing a loved one. The thing about grieving death is the replay of memories of regret. Regrets of not seizing times and opportunities to share, say 'I love you,' ask for forgiveness, etc. usher us into depressive states. Oh, how we wish so badly to have had just a bit more time with that special someone! We try to suppress the memories, but they continue staying afloat to the point where we become submerged. With the hurt and pain comes the evidentiary effects on our minds and well-being. We become short-tempered, isolated, and blame ourselves for what is now out of our hands to correct (if we could have corrected it).

As believers, we are the children Jehovah Roi – The God Who sees. He sees our past in the righteousness of Jesus. All the wrong we have done has been cast away. He sees us as His children in the present as He sees Christ. He sees us with Him in the future just as He sees Christ with Him now. This is an illustration of the ability to visualize that He has planted within each of us. Whether it is a memory or a present or future vision, as His children He passes onto us the ability to see as He does: not holding the regrets and sorrows which torment us, but focusing on the good experienced during the time our loved ones were living among us. He sees them still alive. Guess what? We too can see them still alive in memory and vision – it is the gift of God. He wants us, as His children, to be comforted and at peace, and, most importantly, motivated to continue living life. The physical lives of loved ones we have lost are temporarily separated from us, but the spirit of how they lived and affected our lives has the ability to live on through us. Let us release sorrow and grab hold of Jehovah Roi so that we can look ahead.

## PRAYER

*Jehovah Roi, thank you for truth. Truth of who You are and what You are capable of doing. Truth in recognizing all things serve a purpose, even death. Truth in valuing a mind with memories you have designed and planned for us to utilize. Truth in having those memories to provide an extension of existence, not to ever be deleted but to motivate us in pressing forward. As I give my heart to You and seek Your spiritual comfort and peace, I pray for You to turn my heart against sorrowful regrets and things out of my control. Impart within my heart godly plans to be manifested in actions that carry on the positive aspects of the lost loved ones and let me continue in glorifying You. It seems but a moment that we have people in our lives before death calls, but You have afforded and equipped us with opportunities of visualizing loved ones in a way that motivates us to go forward in living life and looking ahead. I thank You for seeing where I am and helping me to see and appreciate where they are in memory and vision. I bless You, Lord. Amen.*

# Toss the Rope

## Jehovah Selai[1]
## "The Lord My Rock"

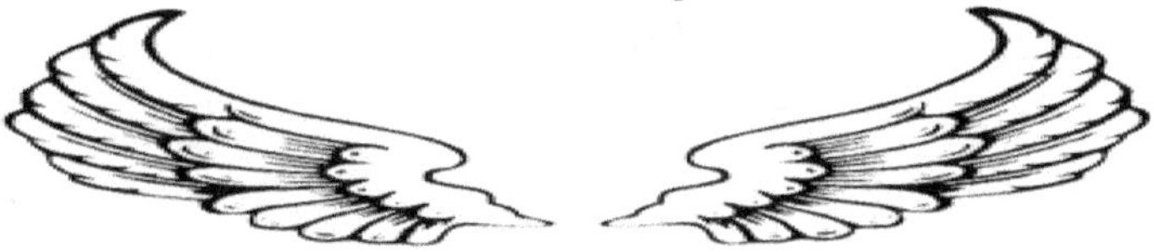

---

*And he said, **The LORD is my rock**, and my fortress, and my deliverer;*
(2 Samuel 22:2, KJV)[2]

---

For most of us, whenever we hear someone say, "I'm at the end of my rope", it means either one of two things: someone is in trouble because the last nerve has been tapped; or all means have been exhausted to get something taken care of. As a child, we would prefer hearing the second over the first anytime. However, as an adult, to say those words means you are at wits end and have no other place to turn. In most cases, we have given all we can give, taken all we could take, borrowed as much as we could borrow, and walked as far we could go – all to no avail. I am reminded of a friend of mine named Harold who was preaching at a church in Arkansas, saying "When you come to the end of your rope, toss it away and grab the hand of Jesus that has been there all along." Nothing could be further from the truth.

Getting to the end of the rope symbolizes you doing all the work – the lifting and the pulling – just to find no one's on the other end of that rope. That is a journey in life many of us find ourselves on, partly because of pride and partly because of ignorance. Pride will not allow us to accept anyone's assistance because maybe we do not want it thrown in our faces at a later time or we want to say we did it alone. Ignorance is simply being unaware of resources available to help us in whatever situation we may find ourselves in – we were merely never made aware of those sources.

As children of God, we must be secure in seeing and having Jehovah Selai visible at all times. With God as our Rock, there are hewn steps in that rock specifically designed to give us a lift. On each step are people whom God set in place to assist us (regardless of their demographic makeup). He is able to use whomever, whenever and however for the benefit of His children, whom He finds pleasure in. His being the Rock crushes despair and is a firm foundation upon which we can stand and build. Release the rope and grab a hold of Jehovah Selai.

## PRAYER

*Lord, here I am stranded and prostrated before You. I have been used and abused by life but that is what it took to bring me to Your feet. States of worthlessness and hopelessness are more than emotional feelings, they are places I have become accustomed to living in spiritually and mentally. In seeking peace and getting on track, I have exhausted every resource and plan imaginable. Now that the resources have been depleted and the track has run out, I find myself by myself facing You. As I kneel, all I am, though not much, I willingly place here before You. In sorrow and shame, I ask Your forgiveness for my choosing to neglect You in an effort to do things my way – grieving You, as I am now in grief. I pray that You have mercy on me and make me anew as I, without reservation, accept Christ –Your word—as my Rock and the governing authority over my life. I need You. I need life. I need a life with You. May Your wisdom guide me in understanding and traveling life's journey. I thank You, I bless You, and, now, I submissively honor You as Jehovah Selai. Amen.*

# Prayers for Guidance

# Life in His Hands

## El Chaiyai[1]
## "God of My Life"

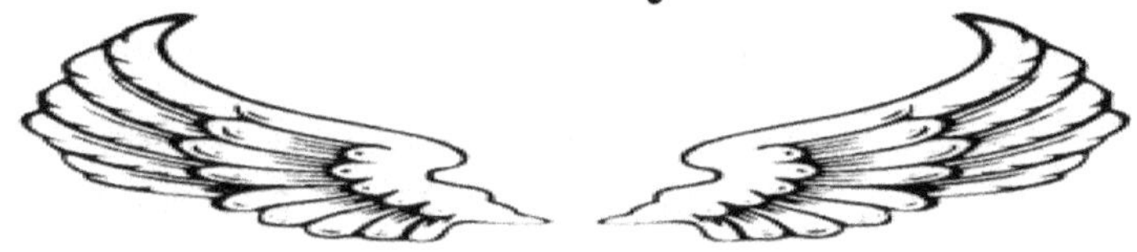

---

*The LORD will command His lovingkindness in the daytime, and in the night His song shall be with me – a prayer to the* ***God of my life****.*
(Psalms 42:8, NKJV) [2]

---

As believers, we should possess and cherish something that is so amazingly beautiful – a relationship with the El Chaiyai (God of my life). What makes this relationship beautifully unique is realizing the fact of His unchanging lovingkindness toward us at all times. No matter the negative or positive extents of where we are in life, He is there loving us and working all things together for our good. Him being the God of our life is not dependent upon how we feel or how things are going on any given day, it is the security of having a healthy continuing relationship with Him. Obtaining such a magnificent relationship comes about when His faithfulness meets our measure of faith. When we exercise our individual measure of faith, as given by Him for communicating with Him, we begin appreciating Him all the more as we grasp His presence throughout our everyday living.

Whatever our concerns are in life, be it purpose, employment, family, finances, etc., we are assured that He is interested in being a part of it. For us to consider Him as God of our lives, we must position Him as priority just as He positions us as His priority. It is a relationship that must be nurtured with communication, hearing, understanding, and appreciation on our part that brings us to where He is positioned to be, speak, and do what is advantageous in our lives. We so easily take for granted His presence and miss out on what He is saying or doing because of us trying to take control of our lives without His input. Let us make it a point to be better, do better, and welcome Him fully into our lives whereby we can then rightfully recognize Him as the El Chaiyaia.

## PRAYER

*Lord, I welcome You as the God of my life by transporting ownership of my life from my hands into Yours. I pray, by the guidance of Your Spirit, to be led into listening with clarity the words You speak and expressing Your love through the character You gave me. Lord, El Chaiyai, may I begin and end every waking day and evening dawn thanking and appreciating You for the fullness of Your presence as well as for this life You allow me to have. The beauty of Your steadfast love is incomparable to any – I pray against being drawn away by anything less. As the God of my life, I am willfully choosing to confer with and represent You daily. Lord, my life is in Your hands – Thank You! Amen!*

# My God

## Eloheeka[1]
## "The Lord Thy God"

---

*I am the **LORD thy God**, which have brought thee out of the land of Egypt, out of the house of bondage. / Thou shalt not bow down thyself to them, nor serve them: for I the **LORD thy God** am a jealous God, visiting the iniquity of the fathers upon the children unto the third and fourth generation of them that hate me; and shewing mercy unto thousands of them that love Me, and keep My commandments. You shall not take the name of the **LORD your God** in vain; for the **LORD** will not hold him guiltless that takes His name in vain.*
(Exodus 20:2, 5-7, KJV)[2]

---

Being human, we each crave, have and/or need personal trusted relationships that benefit all parties mutually. Having that trusted relationship is based on quality and value of the need each person brings to the table of our lives. Those needs are governed by what we lack and require to function in any given area of our lives. Most importantly, that trusted relationship must be reliable and durable in withstanding external attacks, accepting internal honesty, and providing transparency regarding the core need.

So often we put all of our stock into relationships without realizing that no one person was built to handle or value everything about us or fulfill any and every need. Hence, it is to our utmost advantage to know there is but One relationship that is pure and satisfying on every level, and that relationship entails knowing God personally as Eloheeka (The Lord My God). He alone bears the brunt of all our shortcomings, supplies all of our needs, and stands with us throughout the 'good' and 'bad' we encounter. To know Him personally as Eloheeka empowers us to utter the words "My God" when we cry out in times of joy, mourning, or simply in general prayer conversations with Him. Value the established relationship you have with Him above all others and exercise your right to rely on Eloheeka.

## PRAYER

*Eloheeka! May the greatness of Your presence be evident in my everyday life and may I value this relationship beyond any. In You alone can be found trustworthiness. You alone walk every step of our lives with us. You alone possess all we need. You alone are our need. I pray for a heart that stands with bold integrity in refusing to ever take Your name in vain. I pray for a mind and heart that praises and worships you as My God at all times. Name above all names, be glorified and magnified in and through my life. Amen!*

# Reassured Acceptance

## Elohim[1]
## "The Eternal God"

---

*In the beginning **God** created the heavens and the earth.*
(Genesis 1:1, KJV)[2]

---

The best news we as believers could ever receive is the knowledge of God as Elohim (The Eternal God). To our dismay, without the knowledge and understanding of Him being Elohim we remain crippled in our walk. Knowing Him as Elohim helps strengthen our faith and opens our eyes to seeing Him as steadfastly present and unchanging in His love, forgiveness, and acceptance of us as His children. To our disadvantage, the longer we remain blind to this knowledge, the deeper we sink into condemnation from the enemy and stray into doing who knows what for however long. He stands watch eternally over our souls as He heeds and accepts the words of intercession made on our behalf which are spoken by His Son. Being mindful of Him as The Eternal God enhances the odds of us representing well, without condemnation, in the present and in the future. Let us repent and receive Him as Elohim so that He can perform the renovation our lives so desperately need along with an eternal blessed reassurance.

## PRAYER

*Lord, here I am questioning whether or not I'm still considered to be Your child. This question arises out of my misrepresenting You in the actions and lifestyle I have chosen to live: my avoiding You whenever there are opportunities for me to go to church or engage in conversations about You; and my lacking motivation to read Your word or search after you wholeheartedly. For whatever reason that I cannot explain, this day has come and with it a strong urging for me to seek You and seek assurance of acceptance in Christ by You. I know I have been living a life of sin that continually covered the seed of Your word and hope planted within my heart years ago; yet, the seed and hope remains. It is now, upon that seed and hope, that I call out to You in shame, hurt, and tears to say I apologize and ask Your forgiveness. I pray to be made right with You by building on the mustard seed of faith in the sacrifice of Jesus, Your Son, for all my wrong.*

*I pray for an everlasting assurance of being accepted as Your child. In becoming Your child, I surrender my will, ideas of the meaning of life, and self-centeredness at Your feet. As I look to You, I pray for the fullness of Your Spirit to live within me so that I can live for You, that I may know You as Elohim (the eternal God) of my life and purpose forever. I thank You and pray that You will draw me closer to You daily hereafter in Christ and by the leading of Your Spirit. Amen.*

# You're Ready

## Immanuel[1]
## "God With Us"

---

*Therefore the Lord himself shall give you a sign; Behold, a virgin shall conceive, and bear a Son, and shall call* ***His name Immanuel****.*
(Isaiah 7:14, KJV)[2]

---

Have you ever found yourself intuitively and desperately seeking God's will for your life through prayer? Oftentimes that passionate desire and drive is the result of us being equipped by God and with God to do more. In all actually, it is God calling on us to use those talents and gifts He has placed within us. Many times, the talents and gifts are left dormant, not so much intentionally, but because of fear. We fear being embarrassed, ridiculed, and failing. In turn, we put God in the passenger seat and allow fear to do the driving.

Think on it for a moment: we put God (Who is with us), in the passenger seat. We have a powerful, unfailing, faithful God joined with us on the inside and yet we allow a wavering emotion [fear] fill our minds with preconceived negatives that impact our moving forward and hold us idly hostage. Let's repent, turn and kick fear out of the vehicle of our minds, and press into what thus says Immanuel – He is with us to see us through whatever challenge comes our way. While we are kicking fear out of our minds, keep the door for the ejection of pride and any other emotion that impedes our obedience in serving God. Having God with us, we are not only equipped, but we are also ready!

## PRAYER

*Lord, what comforting news it is knowing Immanuel. We are more than ready for the work of the kingdom with You being with us. No longer will I allow fear and pride to dictate the course of my life. I will do whatever is to be done by the power of God, even if I must do it afraid. I will honor the true and all-powerful God whom I serve by giving Him the wheel in times of my unsurety, and I will heed His instructions in doing what I am called and equipped to do. Lead me from pridefully thinking of how I appear before others and the preconceived negative results that I picture. Your work is not about drawing people to me. Your work is about pointing people to You by filling a need in their lives, however You lead. Lord, as You are with me, I pray that You touch my heart and mind to be committed to being with you. Amen.*

# Next Level

## Jehovah El Negamoth[1]
## "God That Revealed"

---

*And the LORD appeared again in Shiloh: for the **LORD revealed Himself** to Samuel in Shiloh by the word of the LORD.*
(1 Samuel 3:21, KJV)[2]

---

Over the years and throughout numerous Bible discussions with other believers, receiving a commonly 'profound' answer to the question "Have you ever read the entire bible?" never failed. That 'profound' answer, as anticipated, was "No." Although there were various reasons among believers as to why they had not read the entire Bible, there was one particular reason that outweighed all others roughly by 98 percent: the Bible was too difficult to read and understand. Interestingly enough, we live in a society that prefers easiness over hard work (which instills responsibility, respect, and morals). Taking the easy route robs us of ever attaining the next level; we want it given to us. All relationships are built on communication. The less the communication, the weaker the relationship, and, likewise, the more communication, the stronger the relationship.

As believers, we can spend 24 hours a day praying for more of God in our lives and not experience it ever happening. Such times will only leave us with memories of excitement experienced in past moments when we initially surrendered and invited Him into our hearts. Getting to that next level of a deeper relationship with Him, whereby He becomes Jehovah El Negamoth, requires us to spend quality time with Him by reading His word, hearing Him speak to us through His word, and actively living His word. It is like any relationship that grants favor to the one who is shown to be committed. Whether it be a job, marriage, or friendship, the onus is on each of us to learn, receive from, and understand the feedback given with regard to what pleases the other person within that relationship, and behave accordingly. When God reveals Himself to us at that next level, we become entrusted and privy to certain information and empowered to carry out next level assignments that baffle others. The deeper the relationship, the more He reveals Himself and provides throughout our everyday life – giving peace within the struggles, promotions during firings, love in a world filled with hate, and strength to overcome whatever weaknesses we have. Take the opportunity to engage with Jehovah El Negamoth well beyond being a stranger.

## PRAYER

*Lord, I bless You for the revelation of needing You. I pray that I will not utter complaints and vain prayers, but instead be silent so that I may seek and hear what thus says the Lord, Jehovah El Negamoth. So often I have been guilty of taking my relationship with You for granted and making it about my needs and wants. I apologize. I humbly ask for You to repair my heart's desire, that I may seek and seize opportunities to spend quality time with You by reading Your word more, being wise about the company I keep, as well as honoring You by how and where I spend my time. I realize that as much as You want to give to Your children, we have not matured enough for receiving it. Lord, forgive us. I pray that You help us to mature by placing a hunger within that awakens us to the knowledge of where we are and the wisdom of where You want us to be. Reign Lord, reign. Keep our eyes affixed upon You on the throne of our lives. Keep our knees bent before Your presence as we worship You. Keep Your spoken word sealed in our hearts. Help us to magnify You in word and deed daily. I bless and thank You. Amen.*

# My Bad

## Jehovah-Makkeh[1]
## "Lord Who Strikes (Disciplines)"

*My eye will not spare, nor will I have pity; I will repay you according to your ways, and your abominations will be in your midst. Then you shall know that* ***I am the LORD who strikes****.*
(Ezekiel 7:9, NKJV)[2]

The cliché 'what goes around, comes around' is what most people I know like to call "karma." Although this cliché can be factual in some cases, it is not entirely true – unless, of course, it is referring to seeds literally being planted in the ground over and over from the same source. Case in point, being good does not prevent something bad from ever happening to you; likewise, doing wrongful activities all your life does not prevent good things from ever happening to you. Here in the good ol' U.S.A., we have a hurried tendency to use clichés and terms associated with *karma* for satisfying our wishes for vengeance when someone has wronged us, even if we or they are believers. Are we assigned watchmen sent by God to be judge and jury all the while offering no mercy or grace? The answer is, 'No.'

Knowing our Father as Jehovah-Makkeh, helps us to understand that there are being consequences for actions in the form of discipline, rather than 'what we did will be done back to us.' Here lies the difference. Discipline sets us on a course of correction, whereas having something done to us that we did to someone else is satisfying the wrong by paying the exact same price. Guess what? Jesus has already paid the price to satisfy all of our sin debts, releasing grace and mercy upon all of us. What we as believers experience now is various forms of discipline that puts and/or keeps us on track with God according to His calling and us having a relationship with Him. When not-so-good things happen, whether by your hands or the hands of someone else, and your conscience is being pricked, look up and thank God that He has not forsaken you – He is just being Jehovah-Makkeh.

## PRAYER

*My God, the Lord Who strikes (disciplines), thank You for not being distant from me in my times of wrongdoing. Thanks for pricking my conscience and getting me back on track. You remind me to forgive, love, do good, etc. as a representation of the Father's character of Whom I am a descendant. I pray against ever having a seared conscience and to be keenly aware of Your presence –*

*having an opportunity to set things right when I have strayed. May stubbornness never have rule over me, nor the power of temptation ever overtake me against Your word. It is upon Your word I stand, I am transformed, and I walk in confidence. In Your discipline there is an extension of love, like a lasso, that brings in Your wandering sheep. Thanks for Your care and watchful eye. Yours forever and always. Amen.*

# He is Here

## Jehovah Shammah[1]
## "The Lord is Present"

*All the way around shall be eighteen thousand cubits; and the name of the city from that day shall be:* ***THE LORD IS THERE****.*
(Ezekiel 48:35, NKJV)[2]

The Christian experience has to be on the top of the list of being one of the most unique unorthodox, but orthodox experiences among all religions. Typically, many of the other religions follow the same pattern and tone of worship worldwide. However, Christianity is comprised of sects of every flavor that appease each type of country, people, faith, race, etc. It could be (and most likely is) viewed as a rather confusing religion when looking in from the outside. But you know what? Regardless of the religious schematics involved, when He is worshipped in spirit and truth, Jehovah Shammah – The Lord is Present.

There is no need for us to shout aloud as though He is somewhere far off from us. As His children, we are privileged to have Him living within our hearts. He is present within. Whether we pray shouting aloud or in a silent whisper, rest assured that He is present. You do not go through the ups and downs of life alone, He is there with you. Though our spirit grows weary at times, His Spirit assures us of His presence to help reenergize and refocus us for the life ahead. With Him being present, all that He is and can do comes along with Him. He can either change the season we are in or provide covering to us for protection. He can silence those coming against us or allow them to continue for the building of our character. His presence makes sense of all we encounter. See to it that you never forget Jehovah Shammah!

## PRAYER

*God, I thank You for being present to hear me, to hear us. The confidence of living for You starts with knowing You are here. Your Spirit guides us in all Your ways. Your word instructs us accordingly. Your ear never goes deaf to the prayers of Your children. Your presence makes all the difference in us being victors or victims. Your presence is our courage. Your presence of truth overrides the lies of the enemies before us. Your presence inspires vision and reveals victory. The beauty of Your presence is nothing less than praiseworthy. In Your presence, we cannot fail as long as our eyes are affixed upon You. Lord, lead us into Your presence in prayer that we may magnify and glorify You as deserving. Amen!*

# Prayers of Self-Identity

# Who Am I?

## Abba[1]
## "Father"

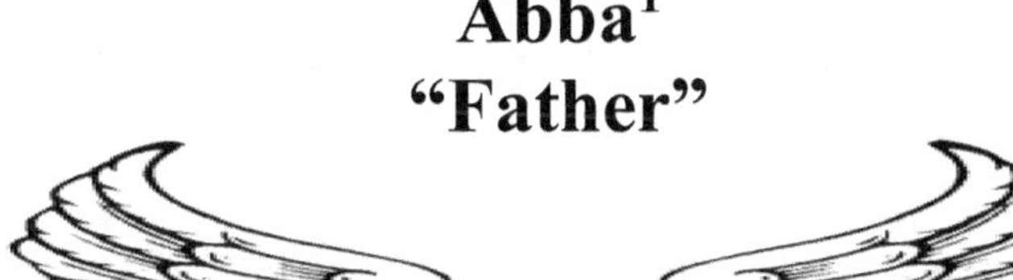

---

*For you did not receive the spirit of bondage again to fear, but you received the Spirit of adoption by whom we cry out, "**Abba, Father**."*
(Romans 8:15, NKJV)[2]

---

The struggle many of us have had or are having is discovering self-identity. We have each been uniquely created and birthed by a Parent who unconditionally loves and has purposed within us the ability to extend that love toward others. Understandably, the problems many face are the errant ways of our natural parents which bring about confusion in our minds when we attempt to make the connection between who we are and/or are striving to become. We have those parents who seek the best for the children. Unfortunately, many parents do not allow their children to grow into their own person by tapping into their God-given purpose – instead, there is a formulated plan and vision for being successful as deemed by the world's view that the parents have mapped out and expect them to follow. On the other hand, we have parents who, sadly, do not show any concern about or involvement with their children or their children's future. In the growing years of these children, they have nothing less than observations of their parents' faults, especially their physical, spiritual, and/or financial absences and neglect, which leads them fending for identity by grabbing hold of whatever can easily be imitated of the actions of others within their environment. On the flipside, there are children who are simply rebellious by nature, intentionally disregarding parental guidance; therefore, they are left to learn the facts of life and gain self-identity by detrimental experiences.

Whatever the route has been for any of us, once we are brought to the knowledge and acceptance of Jesus as Lord over our lives, it is imperative that we continue to mature in our relationship with God so that we come to recognize Him as the blueprint Parent for our complete good. We must recognize Him as Abba (Father). In recognizing Him as Abba (Father), we observe and absorb His words of wisdom – for understanding His love, care, discipline, and character through the guidance of His Spirit which is alive in us. We know that He is aware of our every struggle, disappointment, and short-coming because our big brother, Jesus, not only faced and overcame the same, but provided an unflawed example for us to discover our own self-identity. That self-identity is found in the wondrous working power of His spirit operating in and through our lives fulfilling purpose at every turn in our lives. Knowing who we are and Whose we are becomes a discovered self-identity that will open doors for seizing unimaginable opportunities and positions in our lives which will each serve a purpose for an appointed time.

## PRAYER

*Abba (Father), I thank you for being the ultimate Parent. Wrapped in confusion, I accepted whatever about myself. In doing so, I've become stuck in this state of confusion – not knowing who I am, where this all started, nor how to break free. All the while others, who are just as confused and lost as I am, cheered me on and made this a comfortable state of being. However, something within would not give way to the peace I needed. I am now brought to a brink of destruction and needing to find who I really am. The seed of your Word was planted in me during my younger years from going to church and hearing about You, and was watered throughout the years by Christian artists, television programs, friends, family, etc. Now here I am, standing in need of truth about my identity. I urgently need You for answers. I admit openly and honestly before You that I am a mess! I am lost and I need deliverance. Lord, please have mercy on me! Forgive me for neglecting You by walking in a 'know-it-all' attitude, casting You aside. Who am I to hide from Your presence or to even think I am capable of moving You out of my life? Lord, I now know that You are here at all times and that it was sin that deceived me in hiding from You. As I come to You at this moment and offer who I have become at the feet of the cross, I pray for a breakthrough, for change to become who You would have me to be. It is in the sacrifice of Christ that I am able to connect with the Father's love and mercy that I may obtain peace, purpose, and an identity of truth. Help me in becoming Your child – to hunger, thirst, and cry after You, being filled by Your daily bread. I profess and represent You this day forward as Abba. May Your Holy Spirit strip the filth of sin from me and cleanse me by your Word. Have Your way, Lord, have Your way this day and forever, I pray. Amen.*

# Sober Up!

## El Yalad[1]
## "God Who Gave You Birth"

---

***Of the Rock who begot you**, you are unmindful, and have forgotten the **God who fathered you**.*
(Deuteronomy 32:18, NKJV)[2]

---

Upon joining the military, regardless of which branch of service, each person must undergo an indoctrination and transformation process which serves the purpose of stripping individual norms and re-equipping with a unification concept of good order and discipline for achieving mission success. During the re-equipping phase, pride, honor, respect, mores, and integrity are instilled in each member along with expectations of representation of each branch of service. Those expectations of representation separate military members from common members of society. Whether it is by observation of behavior, speech, walk, or character, many civilians in society are very good at identifying whether or not someone out of uniform is a military member. Many will agree that one sure way a mistake in identity may occur is when the military member does something questionable that brings discredit upon self and the service.

Much like the military, we as believers undergo a make-over process starting the moment we sincerely surrender and accept Christ into our lives. With that make-over comes an expectation of a godly transformation. Unfortunately and all too often that transformation is derailed due to many believers operating based on worldly conformism [believing it is acceptable to proclaim Christianity but live an opposite lifestyle]. Hypocritical behavior not only stumps or weakens the faith of others who are sincerely in search of Christian authenticity, it feeds into the fallacy of God lessening His standards to benefit us. Bottom-line is that we need to sober up and remember Whose we are and who we are! When we sincerely invite and accept God into our lives, we are surrendering our will and character for His – meaning He has what we desire; therefore, we are to go through a transformation in order to become. As a believer, I implore you to always be mindful of El Yalad (God Who gave you birth) and represent well.

## PRAYER

*God, I thank You for Your longsuffering, Your calling, and Your birthing, transforming, equipping and expectations of me. I apologize for misrepresenting You by allowing my carnal nature opportunities to take the lead and hinder Your transforming work of creating me anew. It is You who have fathered me and provided instructions by Your word for my benefit. I pray that the planted seed of Your word would take root in my heart and produce spiritual fruit, manifested in my actions, that will benefit others. Let me not be a hindrance to the progress of Your work in the lives of others nor of Your work in my very own life. May my character be completely submerged in honoring You as El Yalad. Blessed be Your name and position over all life forever. Amen!*

# I Know Who I Am

## Jehovah Eli Meleki[1]
## "God My King"

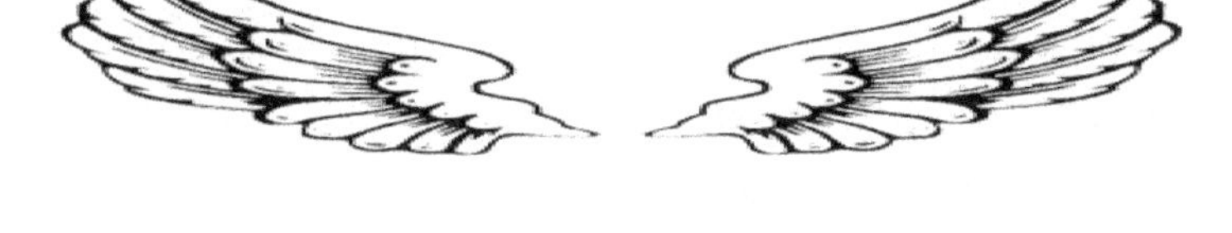

---

*They have seen Your procession, O God, the procession of my God, **my King**, into the sanctuary.*
(Psalms 68:24, KJV)[2]

---

One thing that is most detrimental for any living being to suffer is a death of identity. Having no sense of identity not only thwarts having purpose in your life, but it also diminishes how you view yourself. Wandering about 'trying to find myself' appears to be a common mantra for many in today's generation. Sadly, they do so with good reason, as they have seen poor godly examples from past generations. Wanderers seek to fit in by sticking out in the most negative ways imaginable. Walking by faith has been put on the back burner whereas 'if you see it, you can have or be it' has become the motto that many cling to in defining themselves. They have taken and used their testimonies to exalt themselves as being a 'somebody' who is 'self-made', as they proudly thank God for endorsing their ungodly behaviors. However the cake is sliced, it is not a cake without the crowning layer of icing (i.e., God).

For us to personally recognize God as King of our lives, we must be willing to undergo a renovated identity. The process involves knowing Him by having a personal relationship with Him. The more time we spend with Him, the stronger our faith becomes and the more our identity meshes with His (which adds tremendous value to our identity). Our identity becomes shaped by following after Him and the leading of His Spirit within us. We slowly but surely begin walking more and more by faith and less by what we see in the natural. We realize Jehovah Eli Meleki renders the 'self-made' philosophy as void. We begin humbly operating as kings and priests (Revelation 1:6), a royal priesthood and a peculiar people (1 Peter 2:9) filling a greater purpose beyond the "I' mentality.

## PRAYER

*God my King – Jehovah Eli Meleki! I have suffered from a false view of myself and my self-worth. I have bought into an ungodly mindset brought on by the depreciative words spoken about me and around me. As Esau surrendered his birthright to Jacob, I have exchanged my godly birthright for the words and judgments perpetrated by the godless of this world. Now I am suffering the consequences of feeling abandoned and worthless. Lord, it is in my hurt, pain, and regret, that I ask for Your forgiveness and mercy: I ask Your forgiveness and mercy in excusing me for valuing the opinion of others above Your word of truth; I ask Your forgiveness and mercy for yielding to lies; I ask Your forgiveness and mercy for thinking I know better than You. Please grant me Your forgiveness and mercy as requested. Thank you. In receiving Your forgiveness and mercy, I now ask for Your grace: grace to be repositioned in royalty as I accept You as my Father and God my King; and grace to no longer wear the cloak of sorrow and worthlessness but to have an unwavering mind and heart, knowing Whose I am and who I am. By accepting Your grace, I also accept the power of Your love and Spirit to guide me daily as Your steward and child in all righteousness. May this day of rebirth be honored and cherished unto Your glory. Thanks for Your blessings. Amen.*

# Brought Back to My Senses

## Jehovah Go'Eleck[1]
## "The Lord is My Redeemer"

---

*Let the words of my mouth, and the meditation of my heart, be acceptable in Your sight, O* ***LORD****, my strength, and* ***my redeemer****.*
(Psalms 19:14, KJV)[2]

---

How many of us can honestly attest to having done something against our better judgement that resulted in our shame, unwanted consequences, as well as the need for God to bring us out and back to our senses? I am confident in saying we all have. A personal testimony of mine that I will share involved my infatuation with a particular lady back in 2007. She was nice in every way. However, as much as I wanted to be with her, she rejected me at every turn. I did not give up so easily, partly due to a couple of mutual friends of ours continually feeding me information about her really liking to spend time with me, but possibly playing 'hard to get.'

I spent a great amount of time chasing and spending time with her by going out on lunch, dinner, and movie 'dates', attending and planning church functions together, and allowing our children to swap spending nights together with each of us. I was so enamored by this lady that any time another female would find an interest in me, I would easily brush them off without giving it a second thought. Well, after some time had passed and much prayer, God slowly began shifting my attention more on Him, which opened my eyes to see that this lady was not the one for me. I felt so ashamed and disappointed because of all the time I spent with her that I was beginning to see it as a waste.

I would soon come to know that nothing is a waste with God. A few years had gone by and I really had not been on the dating scene much, so I had been dedicating my time and attention to God, my two children, and work. It was during that time that God revealed that the time I spent chasing after that young lady actually worked in my favor to keep me from linking up with any of those other potentials as mates. People who we may think have wasted our time intentionally or unintentionally, were simply appointed placeholders by God. Furthermore, all that time preserved and readied me for something more glorious which I had not seen coming – the meeting and marrying of my lovely wife, Ramona.

When we shift our attention to Jehovah Go'Eleck, He readies us for a presentation of the desires of our hearts by redeeming any and everything we have ever lost. We go from shame and disappointment to becoming an humble testimony to the world, if to say, "Look at God and look at me now!" We go from viewing time as being wasted to understanding we were on His time. We go from what we thought was good for us to receiving what He has, which is best for us. When the Lord is your Redeemer, truly all things will work together for your good.

## PRAYER

*Lord, I am ever ecstatic to proclaim You as Jehovah Go'Eleck! In those moments of chasing after what I wanted, You were preserving me for what You had for me. With You there is never a loss because You are the Redeemer Who lives. You uphold each of Your children through turbulent and dark phases of our lives – allowing us opportunities to exhaust all our efforts. Those fruitless opportunities had to occur first in order for our redemption to follow. Upon You bringing us to our senses, by showing evidence of our fruitless actions, we discover that our only need is You. You remove the shame and disappointments that condemn us. You restore the losses and desires as You work within us according to Your will and for Your glory. In You lies all our needs and by You we are fully redeemed in righteousness. Lord, You are my Redeemer, in Whom my life is planted. Lord, I pray for You to have Your way by taking all of me and my mess-ups and turning them around as a benefit for Your kingdom. I shall bless You with praise and worship each day. Amen.*

# Don't Take the Conversation Personal

## Jehovah Mekadishkem[1]
## "The Lord Sanctifier"

*"Speak also to the children of Israel, saying: "Surely My sabbaths you shall keep, for it is a sign between Me and you throughout your generations, that you may know that* ***I am the LORD who sanctifies you****..."*
(Exodus 31:13, NKJV)[2]

Oftentimes we get tripped up taking other people's opinions and actions to heart. When such happens, we allow our flesh to rise up in defense mode which can hinder our testimony and a prime opportunity to wisely share the gospel. I was personally reminded of such an occasion recently. While at the office where I'm employed, a co-worker came in stating that he's taking a day of absence to go buy tons of ammunition and weapons due to a supposed 2nd Amendment change coming down the pipe to strip gun owners of weapons and ammunition, as heard on an extreme conservative news outlet. As soon as the individual made that statement, I immediately became defensive and piped in that there wasn't any truth to that story and questioned the purpose of having to buy a load of weaponry. He shockingly looked me in the eye, and quickly departed from my office space. Within seconds of his departing, I intuitively knew I offended him. I allowed myself to be on the defense by getting wrapped up in someone else's personal and unharmful decisions and beliefs.

That day, I learned as a believer that I was not only the offender and defender but had also become the judge between good and evil. That is when I had to cry out to the Lord by remembering and recognizing Him as the Sanctifier. As the Sanctifier, He does not position His children to remain judgmental in the flesh but to have compassion and walk wisely by seizing opportunities to share His love. It's okay to have general conversations with others about their opinions and beliefs – it's called "meeting them where they are" for the purpose of forming a relationship of trust. However, the key is not to become entangled in the spiritual enemy's trap of selfishly offending or defending our personal [carnal] opinions, beliefs, and agendas to the point of severing a possible relationship and/or missing an opportunity for presenting the commissioned good news. Residing in the Lord's sanctification enables us to concentrate on the bigger and more meaningful picture of His plan rather than the carnal fights of good and evil. Sanctification metaphorically serves as the believer's Sabbath, representing us resting in God and establishing us as God's sign to others of change and being a peculiar people.

## PRAYER

*Heavenly Father, Jehovah Mekadishkem, I seek after You for sanctification. Sanctification that strips me of judging others and being ignorantly and unfruitfully opinionated. I pray for Your sanctification that perfects me in satisfying Your purpose and will for my life – to walk with compassion and be an example of Your love. I have given my life to You verbally; however, I surrender wholeheartedly unto Your glory for Your working and calling in the lives of others. Lord, as I partake of your word daily and it becomes my lifestyle, may the fruit of it serve as a testimony of your sanctification to those impacted and called by you. Amen*

# Preach Through My Character

## Jehovah Ra'ah[1]
## "The Lord is My Shepherd"

***The LORD is my shepherd****; I shall not want.*
(Psalms 23:1, KJV)[2]

My goodness, what a life I must thank God for! I repented and confessed my sins, accepted Jesus as Lord, gave my heart to God, and was baptized. Now I can go about life as usual. I can still cuss folks out, get drunk and party hard, lie, cheat, and steal, continue having multiple love affairs, and even wreak havoc on social media by gossiping about everybody's business. I can freely do all of this without any concern of consequences because I am God's property. Nope, no weapon formed against me shall prosper and nobody better say anything negative about my God.

A bit of extreme analogy, but I am quite sure we all get the point because we have either witnessed it in others or, at some point in our past lives, possessed this mentality ourselves. Such thought processes represent the moniker of 'a hypocrite.' The truth is, when we truly become believers of God, we also become followers of Him. We accept Him as Jehovah Ra'ah – The Lord is my Shepherd. That entails us yielding the lead to His Spirit within us to guide, convict, and discipline us for the course we are now traveling. If we can continue doing any of the things mentioned in the analogy without conviction, we need to seriously question the status of our relationship with God.

What we communicate in thought, word, and deed preaches aloud Who we are representing. This is one reason there is so much confusion within religion, especially Christianity. Christianity seems to be the most tolerant, "anything goes" type of religion. Nothing can be further from the truth of what Christianity actually is. Christianity is a renewed lifestyle that preaches God's love, grace, mercy and so much more through our character. We are no longer missing in action; we are on a mission for showing the world that Jesus is alive and still cares for and is open to saving souls. Let us not bring shame to His name nor devalue the honorable state of Christianity. If Jehovah Ra'ah is true for you, follow in actions, not just words.

## PRAYER

*Jehovah Ra'ah above all, I love You. I love Your word and truth. I love Your presence in Spirit. I love the fact of You loving someone like me, unworthy in the natural but made acceptable by the sacrifice of Your only begotten son,*

*Jesus. I love You and am ever thankful for You, my Shepherd. I ask Your forgiveness of me forgetting who I am as Your child. I pray for a complete release of the person I was and a stronger hold of who You are creating me to be. I pray for Your strength, words, and guidance to share Your gospel through my lifestyle. The good news of You is needed to penetrate hearts and change lives unto salvation. I am in need of You daily that I may be a righteous steward, sharing Your good news. As my Shepherd, I pray for Your help in recognizing and seizing opportunities for sharing Your word, presenting it plainly and simply, yet effectively. It all starts with how I live more so than what I say. Let me not be led astray by the fleshly temptations of yesterday but by the Spirit of today and forever. Fix my hearing, mind, and heart upon You that I may follow the lead of my Shepherd. I give myself to You and pray for You to use my life for the living and sharing of your word. My Shepherd, my Lord, this I pray. Amen.*

# Sin Less

## Paraklētos[1]
## "Advocate"

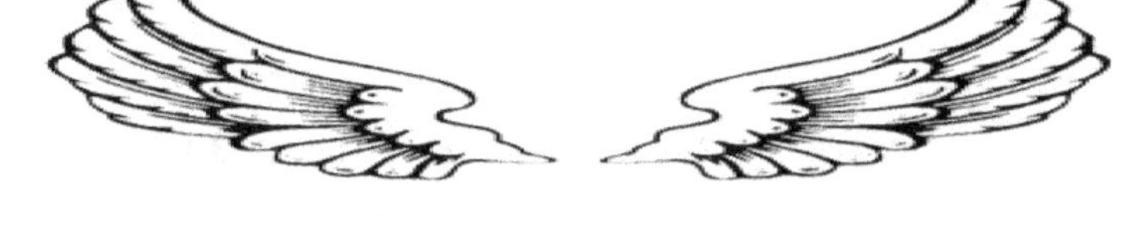

---

*My little children, these things I write to you, so that you may not sin. And if anyone sins, we have an **Advocate** with the Father, **Jesus Christ the righteous**.*
(1 John 2:1, NKJV)[2]

---

From what I have been told by family and friends who have found themselves standing before a judge, there is nothing worse than having an ill-prepared public defender representing you. This is not to say that having a public defender is as bad as portrayed by the experiences of some. Most are overworked, understaffed, underpaid, and all their clients are proclaiming innocence, even when they know they are wrong. On the contrary, when there is a preponderance of evidence against someone and no monetary support from the defendant, most public defenders seem to forego thorough investigations, lack sympathy and any motivation of fair and proper representation. This can make for a bad day on part of the defendant and cost them more than they are able and willing to pay – especially if they are in the right.

Unlike a public defender or any attorney, Jesus is prepared to handle our cases on a whim. He is not overworked, understaffed, or underpaid. He does not have to take time to familiarize Himself with our records. Although there are mounds of evidence against us for clear convictions, He has counterevidence written in His blood that supports our innocence. He has a record of 100 percent acquittals and has never lost rest because of worry. He not only has the Judge's ear on all cases, but He is also the Son of the Judge. With Him as our Advocate, we cannot ever lose. With Him as our Advocate, our appreciation is shown by us sinning less because of the power of His Spirit within us that He provides. He is the untouchable, untainted, and unfailing Paraklētos!

## PRAYER

*Father, it is good to know there is no requirement for me to be perfect – which I am incapable of ever achieving – but because of Christ I am presented before You as perfected. I am free from legalism and free to live life to the fullest with a godly purpose. With all the mistakes and wrong I do; I have the Advocate of all advocates pleading for and having my case dismissed. No more shall condemnation bind my thoughts nor regrets hinder my forward movement. I have been given the pass of forgiveness that allows me to live without weights of sin and to do better in building a testimony onto Your glory. With such a testimony comes the ability of touching hearts and changing lives by Your leading. As the Advocate, Jesus, stands interceding on my behalf, I pray that I will emulate the same on behalf of others in need of You. As Your love breaks through, may we disavow any habitual practices of and/or inclinations to sin. Less sin, more of You in honor of our Advocate. Amen.*

# Friendly Reminder

## Re′u′el[1]
## "Friend of God"

---

*And the Scripture was fulfilled which says, "Abraham believed God, and it was accounted to him for righteousness." And he was called the* ***friend of God****.*
(James 2:23, NKJV) [2]

---

It is one thing to be a friend, but it is quite different to find or have a friend. There have been times when I have been [and continue to be] a friend to others but it was not reciprocated when I needed them. It is all part of the life lessons that we learn along the way. To count someone as a friend, there is a higher level of loyalty expected that surpasses being mere acquaintances or biological relatives. Being a complete and true friend encompasses many attributes: understanding, reliable, honest, trustworthy, and, if need be, willing to give their last. 'Friend' is a term I generally do not use loosely with any- and everyone. Now here is something else to consider when assessing someone as a 'friend': not all friends have all the attributes mentioned. In such cases, I consider them to fit into 'compartmentalized' categories of being a friend. In other words, their friendship serves a useful purpose in your life in an area they are able to handle with integrity. You cannot tell, trust, nor depend on them for everything – only certain things. We each must know the extent of their ability to help before disclosing information to them that may destroy the relationship; we cannot operate from a place of ignorance of knowing (i.e., not knowing our audience).

Unlike people whom we seek and choose to be friends with (which can be proven to be tiresome and disappointing at times), we have a God Who is our Friend. His character is comprised of all the attributes mentioned above and so much more. He does not hold our secrets as collateral against us. He does not look down upon us and broadcast our faults and flaws before the world. He does not pretend to care. He is Who He is, our Friend. Likewise, He would love for us to be His friend. You may ask, 'How so?' Simply by utilizing our faith for believing and trusting in Him. Believing and trusting that He has bridged the gap between us and Him by the sacrifice of His only Son. Believing and trusting we are reconciled in relationship with Him as His children. Believing and trusting we can call upon Him at anytime. Believing and trusting He is faithful. Let us spend time in prayer with Him as friends of God - Re′u′el!

## PRAYER

*Lord, I long to be considered a friend of Yours – such an esteemed honor! I oftentimes feel as though I am not fit for a relationship for many reasons, which I am not going to attempt to expound on. It may be that what I feel or believe is really something totally orchestrated within Your plan for such a time as this, where I am drawn to You. Whatever the reason, I am now bringing this issue before You in prayer for peace, understanding, and assistance in being Your friend as well as having Your strength and wisdom for being friends with others in need. I pray for being secure in who I am, as I have been renewed by You. I pray for understanding of Your process toward my progress in being called Your friend. I pray your assistance in leading me through this desert of loneliness; I have given and trusted, but received brokenness in return among those I have befriended. Grant me wisdom in my selection of friends. Release me from ulterior motives in doing what I do for others; and cleanse me for being a friend with pure acts of kindness toward others. For me to be a friend to others, I know I must first respect and honor my relationship with You, which enables me to emulate what I know of You. Lord, please guide me by Your word each passing day so that my testimony of being a friend of God is evident in my lifestyle and treatment of others. I thank and bless You. Amen.*

# Prayers of Forgiveness

# What Does God Say?

## Jehovah El Emeth[1]
## "The God of Truth"

---

*Into your hand I commit my spirit: You have redeemed me, O* ***LORD God of truth****.*
(Psalms 31:5, NKJV)[2]

---

In 2005, while in the U.S. Navy working at the Pentagon, I was selected for promotion to Chief Petty Officer (E-7). What was supposed to be a joyous occasion took a drastic turn. See, whenever a Sailor is selected to the rank of E-7 in the Navy, it was customary to voluntarily become part of a fraternal induction process in order to be considered a 'genuine' Chief. Well, I reluctantly and successfully endured the first week. However, deep inside I was missing God's peace about going through the rest of the process.

What convinced me to discontinue any further engagements with the group was when one of the instructors made it plain and clear that if anyone drops from the group, they will become like any other, regular E-7 by not getting respect nor help from 'genuine' Chiefs or anyone else in the fleet [i.e., worldwide U.S. Navy]. That's when it hit me that this was not a fraternity I wanted to be a part of. I refuse to be a part of a fraternity that is guided by rules of who can and cannot receive help – being grounded in conscience and faith, I can't but help whoever is in need of help.

Upon dropping out, I was ostracized, criticized, threatened, and mistreated unlike ever before (cannot say 'or after' because a similar situation happened three years later) – this included some of the senior enlisted members ordering subordinates not to provide me customer service within their prospective offices and professions. It was all a disturbing surprise that something like this was happening at the Pentagon and orchestrated by senior enlisted Sailors. It had even gotten to the point where I was told I would not be promoted and never be able to wear the uniform of a Chief Petty Officer. While all of their shenanigans persisted day in and day out, I was yet strengthened and provided the grace by God to walk with unbelievable peace and joy. That peace and joy enabled me to maintain the truth of His character within, allowing me to yet still all of them with respect in spite of how I was being treated by them.

Well, exactly one day prior to the official date of the promotion ceremony for all who were selected to E-7, I was instructed to either stay clear or take a day off so there will not be any distractions from the ceremony. So, I requested the next day off and departed the Pentagon early that afternoon to spend time with my family who had flown in from Texas, specifically for the ceremony I thought I would somehow be a part of. Later that evening, would you believe what happened? I received a phone call from a high-ranking Navy officer at the Pentagon with an apology on behalf of the Navy, asking me if I had my uniform ready to be promoted the next day. He went on to state that a full investigation had been initiated and thanked me for exhibiting character honor, courage, and commitment above all of the news and unfortunate chaos that had just reached his desk.

You may ask yourself, what does that story have to do with "What Does God Say?" My friend, it has everything to do with what God says. In my heart, it was revealed that although mankind selected me in the natural for promotion, it was God saying I was ready for promotion – that was Jehovah El Emeth speaking. Nothing can stop the positioning and proclamation that is spoken of you or over you by the God of Truth. We must commit not only our spirits but our ways unto Him and He will expose us as the testimonial light of His truth through the thunderstorms. All that was ever designed and spoken to condemn you [i.e., lies, defamations, environments, statistics, etc.,] He will use as a glorious testimony for Himself as He brings shame on your enemies by catapulting you miraculously and astronomically right before their very eyes. The lies you endure cannot stop the truth God has placed in you. He has lined it all up in order to show mere mankind what the unstoppable God of Truth makes free, is free indeed. His truth arises out of His children's freedom. Free from what they said about you and your future. Free from hereditary, habitual shortcomings. Free from cowering to whatever and whoever it is that has no authority above God – you are freed by Jehovah El Emeth. He is the Truth that enables you to stand with your head up and moving forward with integrity and character. Jehovah El Emeth empowers us to love, bless, do good, and pray for those who come against us while maintaining our joy and peace. Trust the Truth and be made free!

## PRAYER

*Jehovah El Emeth, I bless and worship You – worthy You are! Thanks for speaking Your word of truth that strips away all that my enemies seek to use against me. Thanks for enabling me to stand in the face of wickedness and wrongdoings. You are the unstoppable Truth! Nothing can withstand the pureness of Your glory. I pray that I am ever mindful of Your word for my life, purpose, and positioning. Let me not tilt the scales in the favor of my enemies by believing what they say over what You have said. Lord, keep my ears open and attentive to Your truth. Help me to walk in Your truth. Touch my heart and lips to live and proclaim Your truth. Forgive me in the weakened moments of my forgetting and strengthen me that I may be made free by Your Truth. Your word of Truth is the power to break, redeem and restore! Thank You forevermore. Amen!*

# You Are His

## Jehovah El-Kanna[1]
## "The Jealous God"

---

*For you shall worship no other god: for* ***the LORD, whose name is Jealous****, is a jealous God...*
(Exodus 34:14, KJV)[2]

---

It is unfortunate how many of us believers give people and things authority over us. Whether it is significant others [people proclaiming they 'love' us but have yet to legally commit], verbally, mentally, and/or physically abusive spouses, positions of status, or material goods, all too often people are sacrificing their walk with God to appease that temporal item of importance. In essence, we make those things and/or people our gods – it/they own us, so that we position ourselves as a second-hand loan to God when it is feasible for our schedule. What trade off could be worth more than our walk and relationship with God? Absolutely nothing! We allow our flesh to be king and queen by feeding its every desire, no matter how unhealthy and toxic it may be to us physically, mentally, and/or spiritually.

Understanding God as Jehovah El-Kanna, we learn that He indeed is a jealous God but not how we perceive jealous to be. He's not looking to bust car windows, stab or cuss someone out, or behave out of character to show how much He loves us. His being jealous is protecting what belongs to Him from the dangers of the enemy that wages war against Him by attacking His children. As believers, the moment we sincerely commit our lives to Him, we become His people and He our God. With that comes the benefits of His protection, love, promises, blessings, and much more.

His protection comes through the convictions of His Holy Spirit within us that serve as a signal or reminder of Whose we are and who we are. His jealousy protects us by maturing us in His strength, His ways, and His character as we walk in a nurturing relationship with Him. Many fail to have that type of relationship with Him because of being comfortable with what is feeding the flesh. It is past time for letting go of the false gods and grabbing hold of The Jealous God – His protection is provided and illustrated in pure and unconditional love.

## PRAYER

*Lord, forgive me for forsaking Your protection for the false security of other gods. Whether it was people or things, there was no security and love provided like You faithfully provide as Jehovah El-Kanna. Foolishly, I wasted time wandering and seeking temporal fixes among false gods. Your grace and mercy have brought me to this point of knowing better and presented me with the opportunity of doing better. I choose this day to do better in knowing and growing in You. Touch my heart, change my ways, and open my eyes as I lay them all at the feet of the cross. I welcome Your Spirit within to awaken me in appreciating and being fed daily by You, and for nurturing this relationship worth surrendering everything for. Thank You for not letting me go too far by calling, cleansing, and presenting me as Your child. I love You and bless You. Amen!*

# Can You Hold Water?

## Jehovah El Magowr[1]
## "The Fountain of Living Waters"

---

*For my people have committed two evils; they have forsaken* ***Me the fountain of living waters****, and hewed them out cisterns, broken cisterns, that can hold no water.*
(Jeremiah 2:13, KJV)[2]

---

There were a couple of catchy songs back in the eighties that parodied gossipers – a rap song by Whodini titled, "Big Mouth" and an R&B song by Timex Social Club titled, "Rumors." Although they were snazzy tunes that charted and sold very well, they were songs of truth about gossipers spreading news to and about any- and everyone. As hilarious as the hooks of the songs were, nothing was further from the truth, especially among believers. The saying from back then still holds true in many churches today, "If you want your business to be known, tell the Pastor, he'll preach about it on Sunday to everyone." Whether it is the Pastor or a congregant, such actions among any believer are foul behaviors. In essence, we become as broken cisterns that cannot hold 'water' – meaning we are good for nothing due to lack of trust.

Recognizing this is happening in our life personally should be a wake-up call to get right with the one we proclaim to represent, by returning to Jehovah El Magowr. As we partake of God's living waters [His word], those leaky cracks begin to get sealed for integrity and usefulness, as we become reformed in the Potter's hands. People love good, juicy gossip but that should be people of the world who do not know the God we know. Let us be identifiably separate within the world so that they will need what we have for their benefit rather than us having what they want for their detriment.

## PRAYER

*Lord, forgive us for straying and giving in to the ways of the world by imitating the world rather than living for You. I pray for our hearts to return to You and for replenishment from Jehovah El Magowr – The Fountain of Living Waters. May our souls cling onto Your refreshing waters of life [Your word], and may our lips speak that which is beneficial in drawing others to You. Let us not be a part of the problem and stand reconciled to You as the solution. Make us over as vessels worthy of carrying Your word by the inner renovation of Your Holy*

*Spirit. Direct our speech and control our tongues as You take charge in cleansing us. May we share that which we receive from You with others, rather than glorifying unrighteous gossip. To live for You requires fuel befitting this vessel for proper operations – fill me up, Lord. This I pray. Amen.*

# They Don't Know

## Jehovah El Nas[1]
## "The Forgiving God"

---

*You answered them, O LORD our God; You were to them **God-Who-Forgives**, though You took vengeance on their deeds.*
(Psalms 99:8, KJV)[2]

---

I have a dear friend named Andrea, whom I have known since 2008. She and I, along with a couple of others, used to hang out after hours in downtown Memphis; whether it was to attend an NBA game, a concert, or even an early radio taping of the Steve Harvey Morning Show, we all enjoyed one another's company tremendously. I remember there being something godly unique about her – she had [and still has] an infectious smile that outshined any turmoil in her life.

During the first couple of years of knowing Andrea, as a friend and prayer partner, I was privy to a turbulent season she was experiencing with her supervisor, who was a senior naval officer. That supervisor would find any and every reason to try and demoralize Andrea. She would shorten her lunch breaks, speak to her in a demeaning manner, attempt to block her from being promoted with intentional poor performance reports full of untruths, and try to hinder her from having any visitors in the office. Those were just minor examples of much more mean-spirited deeds this supervisor doled out on Andrea. Without skipping a beat, Andrea, who truly knows God, continued praying, forgiving, doing, and giving her best every day.

What Andrea understood and acted upon was the vision God had for her life after she accepted His forgiveness. In doing so, she was able to forgive that supervisor and interact with her professionally and with a smile every day. What that supervisor thought she was doing for Andrea's harm, she was obliviously doing for Andrea's good. As that supervisor continued acting with a malicious behavior towards Andrea, unbeknownst to her, she was actually giving God more of a reason to pour favor upon Andrea.

Once the word somehow got around, about issues that Andrea and several others were experiencing with her, making its way to higher ups, that supervisor was immediately removed from her position. And you would not believe how God quickly turned things around and started to rain favor on Andrea in the form of promotions, positions of opportunity, marriage, travel, and so much more that is unimaginable but true! Today, Andrea is not only a naval officer at the rank of Captain in the U.S. Navy, she is a renowned mentor to hundreds of Sailors, traveling the world with her husband, Darryl (who is also a Captain in the Navy), living life to the fullest, and sharing pieces and the peace of God with everyone. With her matchless upbeat and positive attitude, no one could have ever known what she had been through and overcame.

Andrea's testimony came about by her faith in knowing and emulating Jehovah El Nas. She believed and is now evidence of how forgiveness will take you deep into the blessings of God. Understand, her journey did not begin by her being able to forgive, it started when she first accepted God's forgiveness on the cross for her own sins. When we repent and accept His forgiveness, that forgiveness overflows through our lives which enables us to forgive others – that's when God can start refilling your cup with blessings.

## PRAYER

*God of forgiveness, You are. Who has committed no wrong but been unjustly wronged and yet forgave besides You? No one. Who am I, as a sinner, not to forgive being wronged when Christ, Who was sinless, yet forgave all who sin? Nobody. Who am I, as Your child, not to forgive when wronged? A hypocrite. Who am I to be judge, juror, and executioner? A fool. I become nothing more than a disgrace to Your glory whenever I put my feelings and selfish will before Your forgiveness. Lord, open my eyes to see and receive You as Jehovah El Nas [the Forgiving God] that I may mindfully witness the truth of Your forgiveness of my faults. As I am reminded of Christ hanging on the cross and asking for You to "forgive them [sinners] for they know not what they do," I come before You asking for Your strength in my heart so that I can forgive those who have wronged me. How can I ask You to forgive me if I cannot forgive those who wronged me? It will be foolish to even consider. How can I move forward with a godly purpose, knowing I have a heavy sin-burden of unforgiveness to carry? I cannot. I know Your will is for me to forgive but I do ask for Your strength and conviction to do so obediently and genuinely. Let me not foolishly grieve Your Spirit nor bring shame to Your name by refusing and rejecting Your will. Help me to help my enemies, by releasing them of their guilt and into Your hands. In doing so, I understand that I am walking properly as your child by providing them pieces of You and the peace of You by sowing seeds of mercy and forgiveness. Lord, I pray that they become Your increase as You continue leading me in the paths of righteousness for Your name's sake and fulfilling the calling You have on my life. I thank, bless, and love You this day and seek to honor You through the favor of life given to me this day. Amen*

# Justified

## Jehovah Tsidkenu[1]
## "The Lord Our Righteousness"

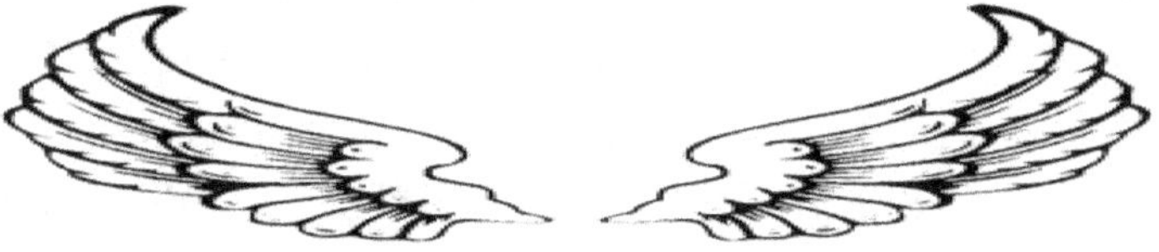

---

*In his days Judah shall be saved, and Israel shall dwell safely: and this is His name whereby He shall be called,* ***THE LORD OUR RIGHTEOUSNESS****.*
(Jeremiah 23:6, KJV)[2]

---

Have you ever been around a person who seems to always be in the wrong, caught doing something wrong, or saying something wrong, yet, always has an excuse to justify all the wrong? Always presenting excuses about it never being their fault, someone making them do it, or just happening to be at the wrong place, at the wrong time and with the wrong company (but they were the one to get caught red-handed!). Guess what? Maybe not to that great of an extent, but many of us were that person and, truth be told, some of us still have not completely shaken that mentality. Legally, there are two conditions wherein a person can be justified for doing something wrong. They can be justified by exoneration of all wrongdoing in a court of law based on insufficient evidence, or if the specific wrong was necessary to prevent loss of life.

In becoming a Christian, both conditions apply to each of us. When we sincerely accept Jesus as our Lord and Savior, we are not only exonerated of all sin, the wrongful death of Christ on the cross was necessary to prevent our loss of life eternally. That alone should make anyone breakout with praise and worship instantaneously! It is because of Jehovah Tsidkenu that we have been justified and validated to be in a right standing with Him. Where our faith is placed makes a world of difference in where we go once we leave this place. Jehovah Tsidkenu is on the throne calling all to be ready to come home before the streetlights of this life go out!

## PRAYER

*How refreshing it is to call upon You, Jehovah Tsidkenu! Your faithfulness to us is reinforced by Your righteousness bestowed upon us. Forever living with Your promises written on our hearts, You set us in Your family and call us Your own. May our desire be to know more of You, the King Who saves and justifies those who belong to You. Help us to stand as Yours in total surrender of our minds, souls, and strength with lifted hands praising You, Jehovah Tsidkenu. There is no other comparable to You nor is there any other worthy of our praise. Your righteousness is the standard barrier that freely separates us from being bound by the temptations of the enemy. It is in Your righteousness where we escape traps set for our harm. Your righteousness is the boundary of grace and mercy towards us. Lord, help fill these temples of ours with words to glorify You in song. Lord, be made known to those who are seeking forgiveness, healing, and justice by touching their hearts. Use Your children to share the Source of righteousness with those who are feeling burnt out on religion and empty promises. Lord, help us to extend Your calling in the lives of those we are in need of being justified in Christ. It is in Your righteousness that we find and have right standing in Christ. Have Your way, Lord, Jehovah Tsidkenu. Amen.*

# Prayers
# of
# Love

# Let's Love

## Elohim Ahavah[1]
## "God Who Loves"

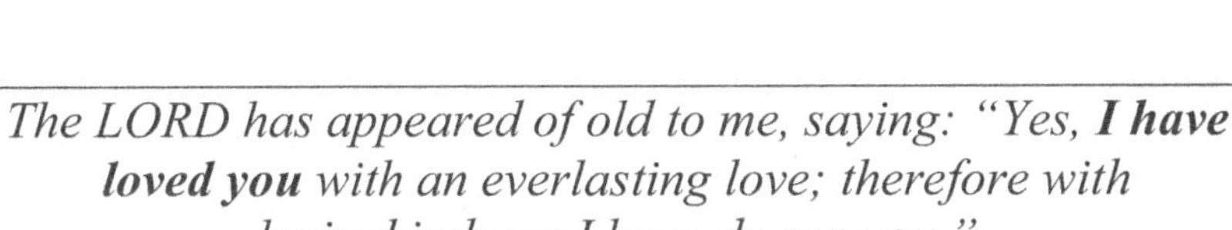

---

*The LORD has appeared of old to me, saying: "Yes,* ***I have loved you*** *with an everlasting love; therefore with lovingkindness I have drawn you."*
(Jeremiah 31:3, NKJV)[2]

---

The one thing that is seemingly impossible to live without, that we learn to receive and provide, and that gives purpose and meaning in life, is called "love". Love is an essential need in our lives. Without love, we are left to operate in whatever it is that benefits our emotional state. Whether we come from an environment where it was not shown in actions, not verbally communicated, or was shown under a misleading guise; or, if the love we once had was taken for granted, used, and abused, it does not mean love is dead or non-existent. As a matter of fact, in the process of becoming a believer we first had to exercise faith by discarding all of our preconceived notions and bad experiences concerning love and accept God's love as shown by the sacrifice of Jesus, which is communicated throughout the Bible. Unbeknownst to us during that moment of acceptance, we were appearing and answering to the call of Elohim Ahayah "God Who loves."

As our relationship with Elohim Ahayah matures, we gradually understand and exhibit His love in our character and through interactions with others. Presently, we live in an age and society where we prefer grouping love as love, without realizing or studying the variations of love; this creates the misinformed view of love being the same across the board. Unfortunately, but fortunately, love can be very complex to comprehend due to various degrees of it. It is unfortunate because as a novice, it means renovating and retooling our trained thoughts and perceptions about love. It is fortunate because it makes us that much better as children of God in moving forward with righteous love and distancing ourselves from facades of love.

In further understanding the working of love in our lives, I feel it is imperative for us to examine four dynamics of love that commonly affects all of us throughout life's journey. Let's take a look at and pray in the areas of where love is most needed: accepting God's love, recognizing love, loving self, and loving others.

### Accepting God's Love

**Love is Agapáō**[1] "willfully and unconditionally finding one's joy in something."

John 3:16 (NLT)[2]: "For this is how God loved the world: He gave His one and only Son, so that everyone who believes in Him will not perish but have eternal life."

## PRAYER

*Heavenly Father, Elohim Ahayah, we so often come to you with our hearts and attention on our issues such that we overlook who You are by failing to comprehend Your love. As proclaimed in your word, You are love. By knowing and accepting this truth, I'd like to simply say "I love You." I love You for who You are, the: Almighty, Redeemer, Healer, Lover of my soul, Provider, Protector, Righteous One, One and only God above all, and so much more! I love You because You are worthy and positioned to receive what You are and continually give to us – Love. I love You because You first loved me, unworthy in and of myself but made worthy in the sight and sacrifice of Jesus. I receive Your love and offer my heart, soul, and strength for loving You in return. Have Your way, Elohim Ahayah! Amen.*

**Recognizing Love**

**Love is Agapé[1]** "charity; love provided by filling what is needed."

1 Corinthians 13:4-7 (NLT)[2]: "Love is patient and kind. Love is not jealous or boastful or proud or rude. It does not demand its own way. It is not irritable, and it keeps no record of being

wronged. It does not rejoice about injustice but rejoices whenever the truth wins out. Love never gives up, never loses faith, is always hopeful, and endures through every circumstance."

## PRAYER

*My God, Elohim Ahayah, thanks for your amazing and undeniable love that is demonstrated in all creation. I pray before You for assistance in recognizing and reflecting true love beyond what I perceive it to be. So often, I am confused about love - what it really is and the depths of it. As I reflect on those times of confusion, which resulted in being used and abused, it becomes clearer and more evident that those were moments where I was at a distance from You. I was merely taking my eyes off of You and buying into either fabricated tales of love or attempts of making love to be whatever pleased me for the time being. I was wrong and I accept Your love and forgiveness in Christ. At this moment, I am surrendering my physical eyes as well as the eyes of my heart to You, that they may be opened to clearly see and accept Your love according to Your will. I pray that You guide my eyes and heart through the wilderness of life's journey. I no longer want to blame nor hinder my heart from loving nor my actions from being lovable. I know I cannot accomplish a change of heart and vision of love in my own power or will. I need and am asking for a refreshing of your Holy Spirit within.*

*I commend the will of my love into Your hands, that I may love when, how, who, what, and where You'd have me, to Your glory. I pray for Your love to quench my daily thirst, providing the nutrients needed for strength and a healthy lifestyle for exhibiting love. God, have Your way by permitting Your love to break through and fill me this day. This I humbly pray. Amen.*

**Loving Self**

**Love is Ahav**[1] "to desire, delight, like, be fond of."

Proverbs 19:8 (NLT)[2]: "To acquire wisdom is to love yourself; people who cherish understanding will prosper."

## PRAYER

*Lord, Elohim Ahayah, I am at a place where I feel void of understanding and accepting love of who I am. I have become an expert at masquerading my feelings of worthlessness and a failure at seeking after You. Running has been the story of my life – seeking love from material possessions, social status, or the 'in-crowd'; it has all amounted to the reality of being at a loss for true love. I've heard about You being Love and have made the decision to seek You as the source for the answer to my need for rightly loving who I am. Considering how You've given Your very own son, Jesus, as a sacrifice for all the wrong I am, is unimaginable; however, I come accepting this as truth. It is in this truth that I pray to receive Your genuine love and instructions of love. Just as You love me as Your child, I pray to look beyond my own faults (which equate to many reasons not to love), open and present my heart to You, and accept Your unconditional love as the needed stroke in the portrait of my life. In loving who I am, I also pray for a personal character makeover that exudes Your love, and is guided by Your Spirit in thought, word and deed. I surrender my heart and life to be a testimony of Your love. This I pray as Your child, for Your purpose, and by Your will. Amen.*

**Loving Others**
**Love is Agapáō**[1] "willfully and unconditionally finding one's joy in something."
Galatians 5:14 (NLT)[2]: "For the whole law can be summed up in this one command: 'Love your neighbor as yourself.'"

## PRAYER

*Elohim Ahayah, I'm calling out to you with a struggle to love. I really need Your attention in touching my heart. In my own strength I try to love when I am wronged but to no avail. I am at wits end of seeking peace with others while possessing a cold heart. Too often I allow the thoughts of what was said or done to rule within, which leaves me filled with bitterness and conditional 'love' (if any at all). I find myself continuously praying for those who have caused me painful harm, but I am realizing that my heart is the source, feeding those vain prayers. I know there is nothing new under the sun and there is no sin Christ did not become the sacrifice for – which includes the unloving sin in my heart I am bringing to You. In believing the extent of Your love for me, I pray for an open-door heart that receives Your love in an abundance of overflow. In that overflow, I pray to love others beyond faults and preferences, without boundaries. I pray for your pure love that forgives others, all the while realizing Your sacrificial love in forgiving me. I pray for love that translates into me helping whomever, whenever, and however, indiscriminately. I am surrendering my will, heart, and mind to you, emptying myself in exchange for a refilling of proper love. I cannot love of my own strength, so I yield and willingly depend on the daily bread of Your Spirit to lead accordingly. I shall forever thank and bless You by representing and sharing Your love wholeheartedly before the world. Amen.*

# May God's Mercy Flow

## Jehovah El-Rachum[1]
## "The Merciful God"

*For* ***the LORD thy God is a merciful God****; He will not forsake you nor destroy you, nor forget the covenant of your fathers which he swore to them.*
(Deuteronomy 4:31, NKJV)[2]

As a pre-believer, maybe for some even as a believer now, we all know how difficult it is/was to have mercy on someone who has wronged us. It was as though that was their mission in life, to tear us down until nothing remained and they had no qualms about doing so – some were even quite comfortably happy in that line of malicious work. All the while, we would tirelessly spend numerous hours and amounts of money to disprove and counter their lies and works of evil, yet still bearing the brunt of stress and health issues because of the toll it had taken on our mental and physical state of being.

The work-around for those who wrong us is to remember those times we have wronged God. We all have – and as long as we are in these fleshly bodies – will continue to, whether intentional or unintentional. God's way of handling wrong is to hear our plea for forgiveness and willingly bestow mercy upon us. Likewise, as much as we would like to, we must not hold grudges but allow that same mercy we received from God an opportunity to flow through us by granting mercy to others. In doing so, if and when they continue to wrong you and I, the repercussions of their actions are in the hands of God for vengeance, based on His discretion. May Jehovah El-Rachum continue to have mercy on us as we have mercy on others.

## PRAYER

*Jehovah El-Rachum, I come before You in prayer for Your forgiveness and strength. I ask Your forgiveness of my failure to represent You and to live accordingly. In all truthfulness, I am and have been for a number of years finding it very difficult to love and forgive others who have wronged me. In my heart I know that is not well with You nor does it represent what I claim to be [i.e., a Christian]. I have prayed to You concerning this matter on multiple occasions before, but at this point I have come to realize that I cannot receive Your answer of peace because I have not allowed the forgiveness You have given me to flow over in forgiving others. Yes, in my heart, I'd rather not love those who have wronged or hurt me in some form or fashion. Truth be known, I'd rather see them fail and suffer to my satisfaction. Having such a heart has not only been an overwhelming burden, but a weight that has stumped my hearing from You, growing in You, and properly representing You. God, I now most certainly know that I cannot, in my own power and strength, bring myself to forgive and love them. That is why I am surrendering to You this very moment. I am yielding my will and allowing Your will to have the right of way in my heart so that I may operate as a vessel of Yours with a forgiving heart toward others. No longer shall I grieve or withhold the working of Your Spirit through me. No longer shall I expect You to forgive me when I have been negligent in forgiving others. Just as You have mercy on me, I pray for a stirring in my heart to do likewise with others. As Your child, I need and welcome Your change in and through my life. Have mercy on me and lead me to extend Your forgiveness and love to others just as You have unto me. Amen.*

# Prayers for Purpose

# Go and Do!

## Adonai[1]
## "Our Sovereign Lord/Master"

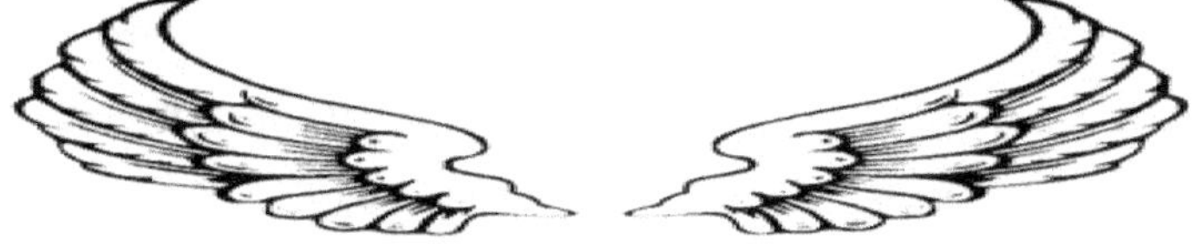

---

*Then Moses said to the* ***LORD****, "O my* ***LORD****, I am not eloquent, neither before nor since You have spoken to Your servant; but I am slow of speech and slow of tongue." / But he said, "O my* ***LORD****, please send by the hand of whomever else You may send."*

(Exodus 4:10, 13, NKJV) [2]

---

Oftentimes we know or have some inkling of what God requires us to do but are quick to procrastinate or make excuses for why we cannot do it. Interestingly, that is our answer after first seeking Him about something to do. In all honesty, it is so easy for us to overshadow His Word and direction with our inadequacies – as though He is depending on us to do what only

He can to accomplish the task at hand. It goes to show that we – including the most faithful believers – can ignorantly possess a very condescending spirit in our communication with and obedience to God.

A personal example of mine occurred in early 1998, upon being in the Navy for 10 years. For a number of months, I had been praying for God to position and use me "according to His will." Well, the time had come. Two weeks prior to the expiration of my contract with the Navy, I was told by a fellow believer and friend (Chris) that I would leave the military and begin a career with the U.S. Postal Service because "God has a new work for me." Upon hearing that information, I quickly denounced it in my prayers and attitude. After all, it was at a time when I was considered and ranked the #1 E-5 Sailor at that particular unit and all the senior enlisted personnel voted for me to be meritoriously advanced; why would God shift me to the U.S. Postal Service and not keep me where I was? If anything needed to be done at the U.S. Postal Service, I was not the guy to do it because I knew nothing about that line of work and had become very comfortable where I was. Well, long story short, God proved He had the final say.

The time came for my meritorious advancement package to be approved by the commanding officer and to everyone's surprise he denied it. What a disappointment for me that was! I was so disappointed that I requested to speak with him personally. He approved the request to speak with me, but I had to wait until he was done flying military aircraft, which was about 11:45pm on a Friday night. We met in his office and he flat out stated that the decision was his to make and he stood by it; and, he recommended I get out of the service [i.e. Navy]. The following

Friday just happened to be the same date as the expiration of my contract with the Navy, so in frustration I decided not to reenlist on Active Duty, got out, and ended up working for the U.S. Postal Service. It was during those times of driving, 50 miles a day to and from the Post Office, that I was often reminded of God being "Adonai" (our Sovereign Lord/Master). My earlier prayers for God to position and use me "according to His will" had different meaning for me when I was praying for them; but, they had a rightful meaning with God as He received them.

As we seek God and His will for our lives, we must be ever-mindful of Him being "Adonai" and be prepared to make necessary adjustments that coincide with His usefulness of us rather than our finding usefulness of Him in our plans.

## PRAYER

*My God, Adonai, who rules above all, blessed be Your name. In ignorance I have attempted to override your works in my life whether it was through fear, self-inadequacies, or thinking the burden was on me alone to complete the task at hand. Then, when things failed to go in accordance with my plan, I blatantly blamed You. Lord forgive me. Open the eyes of my heart and mind to see, accept, and reverence You as Adonai (our Sovereign Lord/Master). I understand that You are not only the orchestrator of the plans You have for me; You are also the caretaker in seeing it through for my good and the good of others. My flaws and weaknesses are set in place as a reminder to walk humbly with You, my Adonai. To You belong the glory, forever! Amen!*

# Quit, No More!

## Alpha & Omega[1]
## "The Beginning and the End"

---

*And He said to me, "It is done! I am the **Alpha** and the **Omega**, the **Beginning** and the **End**. I will give of the fountain of the water of life freely to him who thirsts."*
(Revelation 21:6, NKJV)[2]

---

Many times, we set out on course with full intent of completing a project that we believe God has guided us to do. In the beginning we are full of excitement and eagerness as we gladly put every ounce of effort, time, and strength into it. In our minds we clearly see and try concentrating on the end result daily. We are on fire knowing this is something of God and for God, hallelujah! As time goes on, that enthusiasm and spunky attitude of charging forward "for the sake of the call" slowly starts to wither, leading to worrying and working based on finding time rather than obedience, as the vision of the end result becomes seemingly cloudy and distant. Next thing we know, the project is not much of a priority as it once was, we become disappointed in God and ourselves, and we lose heart altogether.

I have found myself in this predicament all too often, believe it or not, even when it comes to writing these books. It is so easy to accept the mission knowing you are God's person, being used for a specific project to be delivered the unique way He has called and designed for you to perform and construct it. But, as most of us know, whenever God has called us to something, the enemy's job is to bring it to nothing. Well, while I was reading and meditating on a passage in the Bible [John 19:30], three words stuck out to me that Jesus stated, "It is finished." It was in understanding what transpired in the beginning that encouraged Jesus to complete what was purposed for Him and utter those final words. In paraphrasing, there were a few things that kept Him focused on His mission that can probably encourage us as well. He knew who He was representing, He knew it had to be done, He knew it benefitted others [the entire world], and He knew the end result. This knowledge can benefit each of us by seeing God as the Alpha and Omega in every true sense of those words. When He begins a work in, with, or through us, He is there with us to see it through to the end. One hundred percent of the time He has given us something to do, it is for the benefit of others on a much grander scale. Although, obstacles will come our way to hinder or deter, we must remain focused on Him as the Alpha and Omega of the project and trust that He will provide whatever and whomever is needed to assist us along the way. We have favor in the completion of the work as long as we continue pressing forward and relying on Him as the Alpha and Omega.

## PRAYER

*Lord, Alpha and Omega, it is awesome to know You are present in the process. You are faithful to the calling in our lives – may our efforts compliment your faithfulness. In times of losing sight and heart, you were there waiting with mercy and providing grace. I pray for Your stirring to reignite the fire within as in the beginning and stretching it to the finish. As your Spirit resides in me that was in Jesus, I pray for strength towards the day when I too can say "it is finished" unto your glory. Whether the project is being something for me to do or just being here as a testimony, may I unselfishly never cease understanding the picture you're painting is about more than me. In times of feeling like retreating from the call, I declare the reign of my mental state of being and physical abilities to be governed by your word and Holy Spirit. I stand encouraged as the Alpha and Omega is with me, always! Amen!*

# Extend the Rope

## El-Moshaah[1]
## "God Who Saves"

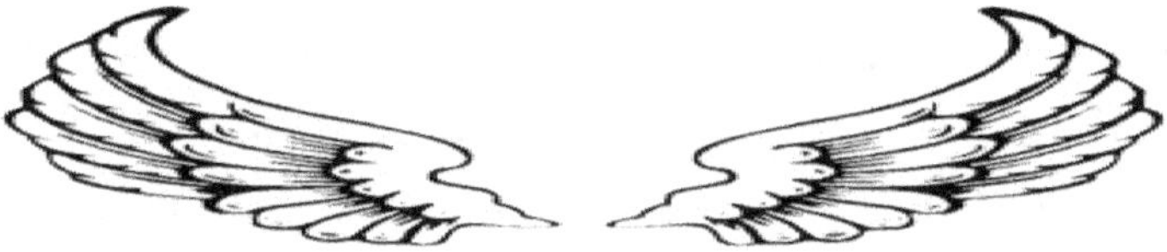

---

*Our God is the **God of salvation**; and to God the Lord belong escapes from death.*
(Psalms 68:20, NKJV)[2]

---

In 1993, I reported to a new unit in the Navy where I met this co-worker who was polar opposite of me. I was a Christian, she was not. I was married, she was single. I am an African American male, she is a Caucasian female. I joined the military to escape my hometown environment and make a career for myself, she joined for a four-year party opportunity to "find herself" (against the advice of her parents). Overall, she was the poster child for being a 'party animal.' She came from a wealthy family (both parents were medical doctors in Florida). I kid you not, every six months during the 2-years I worked with her, her parents would trade out her vehicle for whatever new vehicle she wanted. She was heavily into rave and heavy metal music, had occult symbols tattooed on her back, stomach, and chest areas, did not believe in interracial dating, had no love for the church, and had been indulging in cocaine for a few months prior to separating from the Navy [which she confided in me within a week prior to her being discharged from the Navy]. Knowing all these things about her and she knowing my character as a Christian did not hinder our friendship and platonic love for one another. Over the course of those couple of years during our conversations, she would often ask questions like "What's the big deal about God and why do people waste their time learning that 'stuff'?" Being a novice in Christianity at that time, I would explain the best that I could and provide her with scriptures to read every once in a while. Surprisingly, she would read them and they would become our discussion topics more frequently.

Well, after she departed from the Navy and returned to Florida in 1995, we'd lost contact with one another but she remained in my prayers for a year or so after. Fast forward 10 years later to 2005, as Facebook comes on the scene and people are connecting with one another from the past, I received a friend request from her but with a new last name. Excitedly, I accepted her friend request and we began catching up. She shared the most amazing story about her life after the Navy. A couple of months after departing the Navy, her parents were in a vehicle accident where neither survived. She was an only child and naturally inherited everything. Being in a state of deep depression she proceeded maximizing her indulgence in cocaine and other drugs. Unable to find something to fill that void, she decided to go to this local small multicultural church where on that first day she repented, accepted Jesus into her heart, and dedicated her life to Christ. Furthermore, she quit taking drugs cold turkey that very day, had tattoos removed within a week, met and married a Hispanic male medical doctor within 1-year of being at the church, birthed two children [boys], went to college and became a flight instructor, and she and her husband are both serving as Youth Pastors and are on fire for Jesus. I was floored and in tears after hearing her testimony and God's roundabout work in her life.

I shared a condensed version of her story for the key takeaway of showing how knowing God as El-Moshaah [God Who Saves] enables us to extend the rope of His calling in the lives of others [no matter how far we may perceive them as being beyond salvation]. We are not called to make anyone do anything. We are called to extend that rope of salvation by planting and watering seeds [shared through our lifestyle, prayers, and seizing verbal opportunities as the door opens] and standing back to allow God to give the increase. For many of us, we can look in the mirror at our own lives as examples of realizing He's *God Who Saves*. If you believe He is truly the *God Who Saves*, don't give up sharing that belief with of someone else who is in need of that extended rope of salvation which serves as the call of God on the lives of others.

## PRAYER

*Lord, my El-Moshaah, I thank you for the extended rope of salvation in my life - the rope that came by way of*

*Christ-like examples and years of prayers by whomever you chose to cross my path to plant and water seeds of salvation. To know it was You all along calling out to get my attention and diverting me from the gates of hell, I thank You. It was by any means necessary that Your love moved first to overtake me from the hand of the enemy, feelings of despair, and living aimlessly. You cared with patience because You saw someone worth saving at all cost – I thank you! Help us not to give up on loved ones, friends, family members, and even those who we may consider enemies. Cast us as seeds and water where needed and Lord, receive Your increase. Let us not falsely perceive our presence as the complete package for changing anyone's life and help us to realize we are each serving as needed tools in Your hands. Before we look down on or give up on anyone who may seem a hopeless case, remind us that we were in that same position – out of relationship with You – until, by Your grace and mercy, You extended that same rope of salvation to us, regardless of our condition or circumstances. Thank You, El-Moshaah. Amen!*

# Finding Purpose

## Jehovah Jireh[1]
## "The Lord Our Provider"

---

*And Abraham called the name of the place,* ***The-LORD-Will-Provide****; as it is said to this day, "In the Mount of the LORD it shall be provided."*
(Genesis 22:14, NKJV)[2]

---

Personally, for me, one of the names of God that instills security and peace is Jehovah-Jireh – The Lord Our Provider. I say so because He has never failed nor ceased amazing me during His "show-up" moments. No matter what storms I have encountered, predicaments I found myself in, or hesitant thoughts I had about tomorrow, as I sought Him by faith in prayer, He surely answered, delivered, and remained reliable. When I got out of the Navy in 1998, He blessed me with employment immediately. While working for the Postal Service for four years with plenty of bad experiences, He positioned me as supervisor and officer-in-charge. When I returned to the Navy in 2002, He promoted me immediately. Going through divorce, He sustained me. After divorce, the deaths of relatives, and distresses in the Navy, He brought me out like a champion. After failed relationships, He provided me with a bride He personally put His stamp of approval on, all the while readying me for her as well. Several months prior to retiring from the Navy in 2017, He touched the heart of a company's owner to select me as the Office Manager – a job that was waiting for me to simply walk into upon retiring. No one could ever convince me otherwise about Him.

My purpose has transitioned from 'look at me and what I can do' to 'look at Him and what He has done' – shining the light on Him for salvation of souls first. If you want to find what your purpose is in life, it starts by seeking and walking faithfully with Him. In time, your purpose will be revealed by Jehovah-Jireh's leading and will for Your life.

## PRAYER

*Lord, circles of life have gotten the best of me. Due to my searching for that which will bring me fulfillment of purpose, I have become a jack of all trades but a master of none. I am in a state of unrest with a void that I believe and trust only You can fill. As I reflect on life thus far, I clearly see Your hand at work in protecting, providing, and teaching me accordingly. I am thankful for Your presence throughout. What I have come to learn is that You are the Lord my Provider, and it is proven time after time. While it has easily become the norm for me to take my eyes off of You, I have learned that I need You more than ever. In this learning, I am now seeking You as a provider of direction, so that I may satisfy Your will for my life. I pray to be wrapped and submerged in pleasing You however and wherever You lead. Your goodness has shined on me for many years, even when for the most part I was erroneously valuing and focusing on materialism and status symbols as representing You. I thank You for being in this place of unrest and void. It is a place where I can see and hear You clearly for instructions about what matters most – sharing Your love, in Christ, through word and deed to impact the lives of others. I exchange my thoughts of being a 'Christian' for the relationship of being Your child, depending on You and accepting You as my Father and provider. I pray for You to fill my heart with Your love, strengthen my hands for Your work, open my eyes to see as You see, fill my speech with Your words, and direct my life according to Your will. I bless You and I thank You, as Jehovah Jireh. Amen.*

# Banner Up

## Jehovah Nissi[1]
## "The Lord Our Banner"

---

*And Moses built an* ***altar*** *and called its name,* ***The-LORD-Is-My-Banner;***
(Exodus 17:15, NKJV)[2]

---

Most who study the dynamics and history of wars can expound on the significance of why the charge is led by the one carrying the war flag. In modern times, the tradition continues but with the exception of it not being called a war flag as in times past. Troops around the world carry a battle flag into war that represents that particular country – it serves as an allegiance. That allegiance tells everyone involved in the battle who and what you believe, represent, and are willing to die for – which is understandably why there is little to no tolerance for disrespecting any flag. Just like any flag, there are also personal brandings for businesses, schools, sports, etc. Each promote an "in-it-to-win-it" type attitude, vying for monetary support and consumer loyalty in hopes of surviving, thriving, and becoming dominant above any and all competitors.

As believers, we too are branded. We are branded by the Spirit of God living within us and our allegiance is to Jehovah Nissi – The Lord our Banner. Unlike those of the world, we are not here to conquer and compete, we are here to share the word and love of God with others for an eternal salvation of their souls. We do not and should not go out proclaiming aloud that 'we are better, and this is why' nor have a pompous attitude of being "in-it-to-win-it." This is not a game – and eternal life is at stake. The banner we wave should be seen in our lifestyle – genuine and convincing. When we opt to be like the world [i.e., ungodly and unrighteous living] under the guise of being 'smart fisherman', we are only fooling ourselves and others are easily reading the banner about you as saying, "Look at me, the hypocrite."

Take to heart an understanding that the spiritual enemy of God is truly seeking to kill, steal, and destroy, and we must proclaim daily in our lifestyle "JEHOVAH NISSI" as we charge forward about our Father's business.

## PRAYER

*Lord, thanks for Your wake-up call reminding me of the importance of how I live. I pray to be ever vigilant and always ready for what the day brings by proclaiming You as my Banner by how I live life. It is because of the allegiance I have with You that victory is assured in whatever battle comes my way. It is by the death of Jesus on our behalf that we have an allegiance with You. In having this allegiance, help us to believe, represent, and die daily to self for the benefit of You doing a work through us and in the lives of others whom You are yet calling. This is not to say we cannot have fun; but it is for our good that we are aware of distractions set in place by the enemy to destroy the power of our testimony, in turn hindering others from salvation. Lord, help us, be our Banner in spirit and truth as we live for You. Amen.*

# Light it Up

## Jehovah 'Ori[1]
## "The Lord My Light"

---

*The **LORD is my light** and my salvation; whom shall I fear?*
*The LORD is the strength of my life; of whom shall I be afraid?*
(Psalms 27:1, KJV)[2]

---

It is so easy for anyone to do what is natural to do in darkness – it becomes a comfortable survival mode, both in the natural and spiritual world. What makes a huge of difference in either world is the appearance of light. Light becomes the 'game changer' of recognizing the dissimilarities of wrong and right, good and bad, acceptable and not acceptable, etc. When light enters the equation, the onus is on our individual free will to either remain operating with a mindset of darkness or to cling to learning and being better. Light is the introduction to possibilities of betterment; however, if that light is dim, many would consider it the same as darkness and reject the notion of possibilities as being nothing more than hopeless imagination.

As believers, not only are we to be the light, but we are also to be plugged in and operating from the Source of light - Jehovah 'Ori. The closeness of the relationship we have with Him will be evident in the wattage of light we share among others. Our character will not appear as though we are connected to a blue- or red-light district. The light of our character will be transparent and genuine. It will be encouraging in sparking hope that is attainable. It will shine through the problems of the day and project a brighter future for tomorrow. The light we shine will leave no room for others to guess Whom we represent or where we stand on certain issues. Let us represent the realness of Jehovah 'Ori by lighting it up in our world!

## PRAYER

*Jehovah 'Ori, how glorious is Your shine on me this day. You make all things new, leading me to dream, live, and interact better among and with others. I pray against allowing sin to cause an eclipse between Your shining light in me and others in need. May I reflect Your light toward others as a full moon on a clear night or a distant star shining very bright. You call from among the light, but if the light is dim, confusion sets in. I pray against being lukewarm dim in my daily walk with You. Touch my total being that I may stand ready to share what You have to give. I bless and thank You for speaking through the light of our lives. Amen.*

# Saved at Every Level

## Jehovah Yeshu′ Athai[1]
## "God of Salvation"

---

*The LORD is my rock, and my fortress, and my deliverer; my God, my strength, in whom I will trust; my buckler, and* ***the horn of my salvation****, and my high tower.*
(Psalms 18:2, KJV) [2]

---

Life can be strange in that many of us live it without having any regard for the reality of death we all must face one day. Sadly, the only times many of us ever give thought to life beyond death is during the passing of loved ones. And, as we all know and have heard at funeral after funeral, everyone is seemingly 'going home to be with the Lord.' NOT!!! The truth is, outside of having a relationship with Him there is no other way that anyone can be 'going home to be with Him.' While it is definitely true that no one can say or put someone in heaven or hell, it is also true for me to confidently state that not everyone is going to Heaven as we are made to believe at nearly 99 percent of funerals.

Instead of debating who will or will not be going to be with God, it will benefit everyone to know for sure by being ready now rather than living as thought tomorrow is promised. There is only one way in and that is through sincerely accepting Jesus as Lord and Savior, which is being presented to everyone by Jehovah Yeshu′ Athai – God of Salvation. The great news about accepting salvation is that it encompasses our lives in totality, including but not limited to physical and financial aspects as well – as we adhere to His biblical principles. Allow Him the opportunity to save you at every level – it will be a life worth living, guaranteed!

## PRAYER

*Jehovah Yeshu' Athai, what a name of surety and joy! There is nothing more frightening than realizing death is coming after your life and that could occur at a moment's notice. As death crept upon us, Your love for us called out in the offering of salvation. You have openly provided us a way out in Christ. In accepting Your salvation, death no longer has power over us for we shall surely rise to live again! Our names are registered in Heaven to live life eternally with You. Your salvation sets the protective perimeters about us against our enemies. Your salvation fulfills our every need within. Our testimony is sealed because of Your salvation. Let us rejoice and be encouraged. Let us shine forth the hope of salvation for others. The God of Salvation is welcoming to all who seek, ask, and knock. His salvation is not limited to eternal life only, but extends to all aspects of our lives. He restores hope and renews life. He meets our every need and provides for an abundant life. He not only provides salvation, He is salvation! Lord, thank you for being the Way, Truth, and Life. Amen.*

# Prayers for Meeting Needs

# Totally Complete

## Di Ou Ta Panta[1]
## "My Everything"

---

*But to us there is but* ***one God, the Father, of whom are all things, and we in him****; and* ***one Lord Jesus Christ, by whom are all things, and we by Him****.*
(1 Corinthians 8:6, KJV)[2]

---

Have you ever been in your feelings about being in lack? Whether the situation surrounded finances, love, appreciation, relationships, time, etc., lack is something at some point in life we all encounter in some form or another. The problem lies in how we allow lack to affect our attitudes and our mentality going forward. For some, they get set in regret and bleakness and lose all motivation toward a promising vision in life they once held onto. For others, nothing is ever enough, and they continue to strive for more of whatever.

Whether the concentration of being in lack is due to fear or motivation, we must not empower it to do the driving of our lives. Whenever the feeling of being in a state of lack comes upon us, we must make time to recognize Whose children we are and position ourselves to personally see God as "Di Ou Ta Panta" (My Everything). Seeing Him as our everything fills those voids of lack because He personally becomes our I AM THAT I AM – meaning everything for any and every situation. Whatever is needed can be and is found in Him. As we humble ourselves, repent (sincerely turn from our part of what got us where we are), forgive others, and seek Him, we can then have our eyes uncovered as we approach Him with utmost appreciation of being our everything. He becomes the rope for pulling us out of mistakes that got us in the mess we are in. He becomes our financial manager for misuse of finances. Feeling lonely? He positions Himself through others alongside us. In times of lack, as we draw closer to Him and sense His presence about us, we will each personally automatically begin joyfully crying out "Di Ou Ta Panta" (My Everything)!

## PRAYER

*God, oh how thankful I am for your presence in my life. To see and know you personally as Di Ou Ta Panta (My Everything), no longer do I fear nor am I motivated by fear, for You are Lord of all. Let not this proclamation be for this day and time only but for all times. As I set my thoughts on You, may You keep me focused and secured with a lifestyle not driven by lack but driven by the revelation of You being my everything. In You, there is no lack. In You, there is no sorrow. In You, there is no condemnation. In You, there is no lie. In You, there is victory, hope, and a replenishment of all we need. Lord, as I see You as Di Ou Ta Panta (My Everything), I willfully welcome your word to do a work within that I may represent you well. The highest glory is You! Amen.*

# He Has Me Taken Care Of

## El-Shaddai[1]
## "Our All Sufficient/Almighty God"

---

*When Abram was ninety-nine years old, the **LORD** appeared to Abram and said to him, "I am **Almighty God**; walk before Me and be blameless.*
(Genesis 17:1, NKJV)[2]

---

Have you ever experienced living life with all going well until suddenly you find yourself being singled out to take part in an unsolicited fight? I have on several occasions. One that particularly stands out occurred in 2009 while I was in the Navy. To put it briefly, as supervisor, a junior Sailor presented to me an issue of disparity in the unit's distribution of awards as well as shocking information he overheard from a couple of senior administrative officers. Allegedly the officers engaged in a conversation regarding minority officers not being warranted the same high-level equivalent awards as Caucasian officers. As soon as he finished presenting the information to me, I immediately discussed the issue with my supervisor and provided a written statement as requested for further investigation. That was on a Friday afternoon. On Monday, I was called to my supervisor's office and told my services are no longer welcomed at that unit and ordered to move out of the office until I receive transfer orders elsewhere (which occurred 3 months later). I was placed in an office with a computer, no work to do, and told only to check-in and out with the lead enlisted member of that unit. That was the plan of the day, every day, for 3 months.

It was during those 3 months of being ostracized and tucked away alone in an office space, distant from everyone else, that I received comfort from El-Shaddai. See, though I was discarded by the power of man, God was shown to be El-Shaddai (All Sufficient/Almighty) by providing pieces of Himself in the form of Teresa, Mark, Alice, Andrea, and Jeri. When 99.9% of the unit either viewed me as taboo or did not want to risk the same consequences because of being seen with me, they were among the very few to maintain friendships with me, inviting me out for lunch, dinner, and Bible studies, and offering encouraging words and support – that was the appearance and comfort of El-Shaddai showing up to replenish and motivate my soul daily. Just as He has done with me, He does for all His children who walk before Him for the sake of righteousness – He manifests as El-Shaddai in some form or another on our behalf, proving that He is our All Sufficient/Almighty God.

## PRAYER

*Lord, El-Shaddai, it is a great honor to come before You as Your child. I offer up holy hands with praise of thanks for proving Yourself as the Almighty – touching hearts and filling voids in my life. No matter what has been designed to cast us down or trip us up during our life's journey, You intercept in a powerful way that allows for us to continue running the race unscathed. When encouragement is needed and we are feeling lonely, You present Yourself by touching the hearts of others to come alongside and provide for us sufficiently. You are in control and have the final say over our present state as well as its outcome. Whom shall we fear? Whom shall shake our faith in You? No one. In You, we are shielded in the all-sufficiency of Your care and power operating on our behalf. Blessed are You! Amen!*

# Open up and Pour Into

## Elohim Macheslanu[1]
## "God Our Refuge"

---

*Trust in Him at all times; you people; pour out your heart before Him; **God is a refuge for us**.*
(Psalms 62:8, NKJV)[2]

---

What you say can and will be used against you, not only in a court of law, but throughout life. Most of us know how hard it is to find someone worth confiding in, especially when it comes to very personal matters. Being human, it is not beyond any of us, including our closest allies, to judge. And let us not forget how our personal pride stops us from sharing with others who may be well equipped to help us. Lightheartedly, at times we hypothetically share information about 'anonymous' friends who we're 'trying to help' through a personal challenge – knowing all the while, we're speaking of ourselves. Going the 'hypothetical' route helps us fish out the level of trust we can commit to certain people without bringing shame or judgment upon ourselves – it is called 'saving face.' On the contrary, many of us know all too well how whatever is said in secret has a way of creeping out and negatively impacting us throughout life. None of what I have stated is meant to discourage anyone from confiding in trusted family and/or friends – that is not the point I am making. We all need dependable confidants; however, we must understand that as humans, we all come with a risk of disclosing information about one another to the wrong person(s).

Although we are all fallible, there is One who is a surety for trusting – Elohim Macheslanu "God our refuge." As our refuge, there is no question of trust nor is there a risk of information spillage. We can run to Him with our most guarded secrets, issues, and troubles. He is our refuge Who protects from condemnation. In Him, we gain rest and are relieved from carrying overwhelming burdens. He is more than capable of bearing what we pour out before Him as He stands ready to take the load on our behalf. Let us take that leap of faith by pouring into Him as our refuge.

## PRAYER

*Lord, thanks for meeting me here in the secret place where I am freely able to pour my heart out to You. Although I have people in my life I sincerely trust, I know that trust in people only goes to an extent. In You, there is no limit of trust nor of what I can pour out before You without experiencing condemnation. I pray for the priority in my mind of seeking and speaking with You first and foremost. I pray for wisdom to always find security in You as my refuge from the troubles of the world, even within my own mind and soul. Thanks for Your safety and being the bearer of all our burdens. I love and bless you – Elohim Macheslanu! Amen.*

# Just Listen

## Elohim Shama[1]
## "God Who Hears"

*And* ***God heard*** *their groaning, and God remembered His covenant with Abraham, with Isaac, and with Jacob.*
(Exodus 2:24, KJV) [2]

So often we find ourselves wanting quick fixes to predicaments we have created over a length of time. When the fix does not happen in our timing and how we would like for it to occur, we are quick to blame. Oddly, this is common among believers as we carry over that finger-pointing syndrome of displacing blame from ourselves. How many of you remember repeatedly disobeying your parents and finding yourself in the same difficult situation over and over as a child? As the cycled routine goes, we would cry out for our parent's help because for some reason or another, we were determining to do things our way and refusing to learn. That was until our parents grew tired of our disobedience and decided to wisely use those situations as teaching tools by either leaving us to figure it out, allowing us to suffer the consequences of our actions within that predicament, or disciplining us accordingly.

As the ultimate parent of our lives, God hears. He knows the entirety of how, when, where, what, and why we got into predicaments. We struggle in wanting to be our own little gods by attempting to manipulate the Originator's design and use of things to our personal satisfaction. Doing so only prolongs God's intervening and deafens His ear to the cry of 'wolf' until He hears the plea of sincerity from our hearts. He never leaves nor forsakes us, but we can't say we do the same in return towards Him. As you call out to God in times of trouble, rest assured that You are heard when there's true repentance and sincerity in the call to Elohim Shama.

## PRAYER

*Lord, Elohim Shama, thank You. Not only are You near but You hear. You hear our cries and pleas for the need of You. You hear our hearts wanting to please You in sincerity. You hear our accepting Your word as truth. Thanks for Your attentiveness and readiness to deliver. In repentance, I say thanks for saving me from life lessons and experiences due to disregarding Your righteous ways. As we are Your people, speak forth Your word into our hearts so that we do not stray by following temptations lain before us. I pray that You hear our cry for the sake of righteousness and deliverance, not only in our lives but also for the lives of our neighbors, every waking day. As I ask for Your ear to be inclined to our voices, I ask that we reciprocate the same towards Your voice. I pray for You to make us mindful of hearing and following You as prescribed in Your word as well as through the wisdom of however, whatever, and whomever You speak through as a conduit. May our voices be unified and serve as a righteous testimony in Your ear proclaiming You as the Way. Amen.*

# Vengeance

## Jehovah Chereb[1]
## "The Lord the Sword"

---

*If I whet **my glittering sword**, and my hand take hold on judgment; **I will render vengeance** to My enemies, and repay those who hate Me.*
(Deuteronomy 32:41, NKJV)[2]

---

In 2020 alone, there has been so much negativity transmitted via the media [i.e., television, radio, newspapers, etc.] unlike any other time over the past 40 years. Though the news has been enlightening about what is going on, there have also been some news sources promoting deceitful accounts to further fuel negativity and division around the world. Hearing all the false negative stories is one thing but it is another thing to witness injustices and mistreatment of certain people based on race. What is even more disheartening is watching videos showing evidence of wrong doings and government officials condoning such lawless and extreme acts of violence against minorities but acquitting those of the majority. The same can be said of mass killings being acceptable within a particular race, but becoming a problem if the killing is done by a person in another race. As believers, we must be mindful that those who do not know [i.e., have a personal relationship with] the Lord are doing what they are designed to do – sinning at its best. Likewise, we as His children should be faithfully doing what we are renewed and created to do – representing Him well.

God is the giver of life and protector against injustices. Though it may appear in the natural that no one is being held accountable for malicious and criminal acts, rest assured that each one shall stand before God to answer – whether they believe in God or not. Let us not be in sorrow and seeking vengeance but have hands to deliver the issue into God's hands and eyes to recognize Him as Jehovah Chereb – The Lord the Sword. He can only dole out vengeance to His enemies on behalf of those who are His, meaning those of us who profess and dedicate our lives to Him and trust in Him. Do not let the media get you riled up to the point of seeking vengeance and forgetting who and Whose You are. Rest assured Jehovah Chereb has the case for action.

## PRAYER

*God, it has been and still is difficult to witness the wicked being pardoned of injustices day in and out. In my heart, I really want to see justice being what it proclaims to be, but*

*I know it cannot be so in this world nor can it provide a peaceful resolution within my heart. I pray that You remove the barriers from my mind and heart that keep me from praying for, loving, blessing, and doing good to my enemies as instructed within Your word. Touch my heart to forgive and live for the sharing of Your good news as an alternate to the world's negative news. In harboring hate, I only add to the problems we are all experiencing. I am choosing to add to Your kingdom instead. Though the wrongdoers seem to go unchecked, I am choosing to trust You as Jehovah Chereb. You hold time and life in Your hands. You have set times to do whatever You justly choose to do with each life. The battle is Yours. I pray that I will stand as Your soldier of faith, with a testimony to share of Your love, so that the wicked may repent and truly turn to You. May we not lose sight of our purpose and being about our Father's business. Thanks for Your grace and mercy upon my very life; the same shall I extend to others while I remain in the security of knowing You as The Lord the Sword. Amen.*

# Restored

## Jehovah El Ashiyb[1]
## "The Lord My Restorer"

---

***He restoreth my soul**: He leadeth me in the paths of righteousness for His name's sake.*
(Psalms 23:3, KJV)[2]

---

In those desert moments when we feel isolated after being depleted of resources, we tend to come to our senses of remembering God. Not that it is a bad thing to do, but it is something that too many have become accustomed to doing in that order. It gives credence to the adage of losing everything to gain all you need. On the other hand, life happens, and losses occur (whether relationships, jobs, etc.) even in the midst of walking with God – leaving some to question their faith.

However we find ourselves depleted of resources, we mustn't lose faith in knowing Him as the source. Material things come and go but His ability to restore above and beyond is a surety we can depend on. Take time to know Him as Jehovah El Ashiyb "The Lord my Restorer," repent, and stand with confidence, ready to be restored. He is the source for meeting our needs just as much as He is the need for our salvation. Your restoration of a job, food, finances, life, etc. is wrapped in Your remembrance of Jehovah El Ashiby. His answering begins with the restoration of our character. Speak to Him freely by substituting some of the words in the following prayer to make it personal for your individual situation.

## PRAYER

*Lord, I need you in a most urgent way. I am at a loss for meeting the basic needs of life, while swimming in debt and on the verge of hunger and homelessness. I assume responsibility for being where I am because of mismanaging what was entrusted in my hands, which includes depending on my job as an ensured security blanket and/or falsely believing I can make things happen on my own. I deceived no one but myself. Now I stand here humbled and naked before You with nothing to offer other than a sincere, repentant heart seeking after You. I have ignorantly and foolishly looked beyond You long enough just to find myself running to You in this time of need. Lord, help me by having mercy and grace upon me and leading me into accepting Your forgiveness. I have thrown the best of me away, but I believe and trust in Your love for restoring me. I pray to You for the restoring of my heart, mind, and will by Your hands. I pray for a passion to run after You daily, rely on Your word, and appreciate You for Who You are. In Your restoring, I pray for an everlasting imprint on the eyes of my heart to see You as Jehovah-El-Ashiby, yes, 'the Lord my Restorer.' Please guide my words to not fail in worshipping and praising You in my daily walk and lifestyle as a testimony of Your glory. Regardless of how things are now in the natural, I stand thankful for Your blessing of restoration toward a brighter future. Lord let it be so according to Your will for this child of yours, I pray. Amen!*

# Living Onward

## Jehovah El-Chai[1]
## "The Living God"

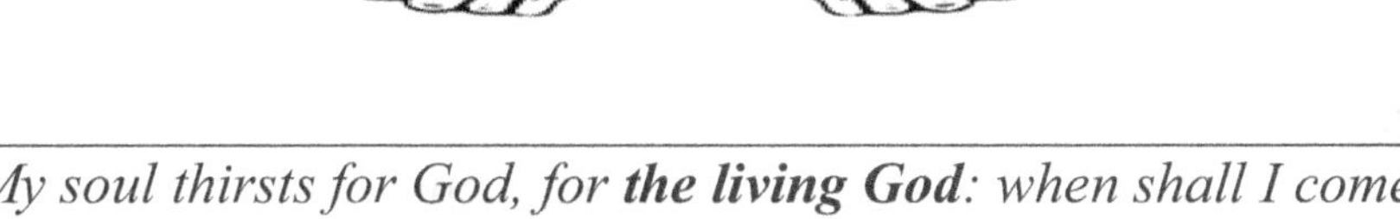

---

*My soul thirsts for God, for* ***the living God****: when shall I come and appear before God?*
(Psalms 42:2, KJV)[2]

---

What can be more encouraging than knowing we serve The Living God? In Him we have the opportunity of living an abundant life in the present and in the life hereafter. As the Living God, He is the author and finisher of life; therefore, whatever He touches springs forth life. Unfortunately, truth be known, when death of loved ones occurs in our lives, many of us go to the island of isolation. Although taking time to grieve can be healthy, it can also become detrimental to our mentality and the fulfilling of purpose when we become comfortable remaining on that island.

Ironically, instead of honoring our lost loved ones, we allow their death to be the cause of our death [i.e. death of friends, living life, hopes, dreams, etc.]. We fail to extend and honor their lives in our character and purpose because we spend so much time wishing and praying for something that's not in God's plan at this time - for them to physically be risen from the dead. However, be comforted in knowing they will rise at the second coming, so life isn't over as you and I may perceive it presently.

Over the past 20 years, I have personally experienced losses of loved ones due to death on nearly every level of kinship (parent, brother, grandparent, uncle, aunt, cousin, etc.) and friendship but I understand that to honor them is to build upon the positive impact they have made in my life – that is one way that I believe God would like for us to commemorate their lives. That's how I envision and accept Jehovah El-Chai breathing motivational life into each of us and through us.

## PRAYER

*Jehovah El-Chai, The Living God, I humbly come before you for relief. With a heavy heart and distorted thinking, I am in much sorrow after the personal loss that has transpired in my life. As stated in Your word, no one knows the day nor the hour but all are appointed to die. The death of anyone takes a piece of life from among those who live – this is the boat I find myself in. I never in a million years could have ever been prepared for such a tragedy as this. My heart is heavy, my spirit is weak and I am at a place where I feel I cannot continue on. There lies the problem – my feeling of being unable to move beyond this moment. I understand that we all have times of grieving and to each his/her own in how long it lasts. But I just cannot seem to shake what I am feeling, living, breathing, and reminded of day in and day out – the memories, pain, and hurt are unbearable, yet I manage to carry them into each newly passing day. Lord, help me! Please help me and grant me favor o see You as the living God that overflows with life to refresh someone like me. I wrestle with pressing forward everyday and am now at a point where I truly need to move forward in life. I surrender my mind, heartaches, feelings of regret and depression, and all other negative thoughts into Your hand. I pray to have the experience of an abundant life that was spoken of by Jesus – a life that is fueled by Your purpose, love, and cherished memories of the lost. I pray that I represent You well by transforming this loss into a means of honoring them and You through my character. Lord, Jehovah El Chai, I pray that You will uplift and utilize the life within me to positively impact others. Thank You for being the Living God, imparting of strength and hope, and drawing me into Your presence for a fresh awakening. I welcome You into my life and give You glory for an abundant life that honors You and is blessed with cherished memories of my loved one. Amen.*

# He's All That

## Jehovah El-Hanun[1]
## "The Gracious God"

---

*And the LORD passed before him, and proclaimed, The LORD,* ***The LORD God, merciful and gracious****, longsuffering, and abounding in goodness and truth…*
(Exodus 34:6, NKJV)[2]

---

Oddly, there are people who not only believe in God but also are disappointed in God. Not-so-good things happen in their lives leading to them feeling as though they are always getting the short end of the stick and God does not care. Their believing expectations are wrapped in God being on their clock rather than seeking and gleaning glimpses of God's grace all along. Ironically, when things get rough, they stray away from the sustaining power of God's presence and hinder themselves from receiving His answers for their circumstances. They no longer attend church, read the Bible, pray, or simply spend quality time conferring with wise people of God [i.e., Pastors/Ministers, true godly friends, etc.]. Instead, they draw back into former ways and crowds that further stumps their maturity in Christ.

Recognizing God's grace is appreciating what He is doing daily in your life rather than the thwarted idea of what you believe He should be doing. Open the eyes of your heart to see His grace in another day of life, His grace in the strength to withstand what comes your way, His grace in providing support within the assembly of His people, and the grace in His faithfulness as He stands ready for you to trust and seek after Him wholeheartedly. To behold His grace is to catch His everyday passing in your life as Jehovah El-Hanun because He is All That and so much more.

## PRAYER

*God of grace, I thank you for Your compassion and kindness. Seeing You as the Sovereign God of Righteousness brings hope within my soul. I pray that we who call upon Your name will recognize You for who You are and what You have given so that we have a right to stand before You and a reason to be ever mindful of Your everyday presence. I ask Your forgiveness for walking blindly and taking You for granted leading to my own detriment with feelings of despair that drive me into depression and a rejection of You. Let us not blame You because of our impatience. I pray that You remove the scales from the eyes of our hearts that we do not miss the sufficiency of Your grace. When things do not go as we would like, help us to stay on course in our purpose, representing You according to the calling You have placed within us. Lead us in Your wisdom to seek and confer with godly people and resources You have set in place for our good. I pray by the comforting power of your Holy Spirit that we maintain our peace with You by not becoming self-centered vessels of bitterness and accept opportunities to mature by reading and heeding Your word. May you continually be present in every step I make, that I may be reminded of why I do what I do. I love You. Amen.*

# Cherish Your Peace

## Jehovah Shalom[1]
## "The Lord Our Peace"

---

*And the **LORD** said unto him, **Peace** be unto you; fear not: you shall not die. Then Gideon built an altar there unto the LORD, and called it **Jehovah-shalom**: unto this day it is yet in Ophrah of the Abiezrites.*
(Judges 6:23, 24, KJV)[2]

---

In 2009, a friend [Chris] of mine was living on cloud nine. He had been reassigned to his dream job location, which happened to be near his long-time lady friend whom he had known since 1993. Near the end of 2009, his lady friend lost her job due to a shut-down and could not afford to pay rent for she and her daughter. Chris, feeling sorry about her circumstances, thought it would be a great idea to have them move in with him -

after all, they were great friends and had already began dating. Around June 2010, he decided to propose to her and she accepted.

Things were going fantastic until a few months later. Since she had not been getting any hits on her resume submissions, they both agreed that she should take a year off from the outside working world, take care of the home, and spend more time with her high school daughter before she graduates and leaves the nest. By her being at home while the daughter was going to school and Chris being at work up to 12 hours a day, her attitude towards him had slowly begun to change until it became a thorn in his side. Whenever he came home from work, she would talk condescendingly to him about crumbs left on the kitchen floor, bathroom lights left on in the morning, hanging his pants over the chair in the bedroom, etc. To make matters worse, as he walked into the house from work, she would leave out to go out with our married friends and return home hours later, about 2-3 times a week.

Upon reaching his wits end, Chris decided to call a mutual friend of ours named Gary. Although Gary was a new brother in Christ, he was wise. As he explained to Gary what was going on, Gary simply replied, "If someone living in your home, whom you are helping out and planning to marry is disturbing your peace, that is not of God."

We as believers so often give people permission to disturb our peace by trying to be the 'good guy or gal.' Yes, we are to be peacemakers and live peaceably among others but never by sacrificing the peace that God has given us in exchange for their misery. Jesus is the only one able to take that deal – which He did – and nailed it to the cross. With God as Jehovah Shalom, He uses us as the calling voice to get others to understand and accept His peace as being what they need, although many reject it. As they continue to reject His peace, let us not allow them to disturb our peace – keep God first by cherishing Jehovah Shalom.

## PRAYER

*Jehovah Shalom! I bless Your holy name and the peace you bring. When troubles abound, You keep us grounded in peace. When we are rejected by those whom we attempt to help, Your peace comforts us. When worries try to drown out the Rock on which we stand, Your peace lifts us with wings to where You are. No matter the circumstance, Your peace cannot be toppled. Thank You for reminding me and keeping me strong through Jehovah Shalom. I pray to not give up on being a peacemaker and to live peaceably among others for Your name's sake. I also ask for Your wisdom and direction to move on from situations that attempt to overthrow the peace You have given me. Lord, reign like never before with an issuance of peace onto Your children so that we may continue being Your voice of calling in the lives of others. Amen.*

# Keep Your Head Up

## Rum Rosh[1]
## "One Who Lifts My Head"

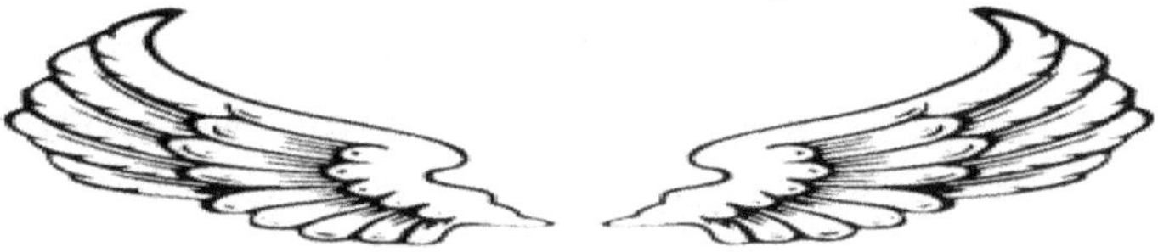

---

*But You, O LORD, are a shield for me, my glory and* ***the One who lifts up my head****.*
(Psalms 3:3, NKJV)[2]

---

It is tough to sell everything as being 'okay' when you have been wronged in some form or fashion, including being mistreated, denied a promotion, lied on, had vows broken, etc. When asked how we are doing, most would quickly respond with the all too familiar line 'Everything is great, couldn't be better.' To avoid shame, we delve deeper into work and find ways to stay aloof from the ongoing world around us. In essence, we are bringing more harm to the injury. We cannot come to a place of healing with our heads aimed downward, concentrating on the injury rather than seeking the proper care needed for recovery.

As believers, our God is Rum Rosh – One Who lifts my head. He is the antidote required when we encounter issues beyond our control. He is not a spectator sitting on the sidelines watching our pity parties in disappointment or sorrow. He is ready to engage but we must first be willing to see Him, and we can only do so by calling on Him. As He speaks to our soul, by the power of His voice alone, we become empowered to lift our heads in response. His word breaks the yoke of any and all things we face. He does not forsake us to find our own way out of slumps, He is the way out. He sticks by us and within us ready to push or pull us from whatever level of despair we are going through. He is not only the Lifter of our heads, He is our Head. It is time to recognize and walk boldly as Rum Rosh leads – unspeakable joy awaits to overcome the source of our stress.

## PRAYER

*Lord, I need to see You as Rum Rosh during this season of my life. I have been beating myself up with guilt and shame brought on by things out of my control. I feel as though I am a failure, and my hopes and dreams have all faded. The worries and shame are unbearable burdens I know You would not have me to carry, but I cannot keep from picking them up. Forgive me for having wavering trust in You. The wavering is a result of me keeping my head down and remaining distant from You because of how I picture You seeing me – which is a picture painted by the enemy to distract and destroy my faith in You. In the Spirit You have spoken to me, that now is the time to run to You, which brings me to this prayer. I pray for relief of the burdens of worry and shame. I pray to be strengthened and healed by Your Spirit of comfort. Help me to find security in You so that I no longer masquerade, but live what is true. You are the God of justice and already have a plan in action to recover and restore the unspeakable joy You alone are able to provide. I shall stand steadfast in Your deliverance and Your word. I receive You as Rum Rosh and shall boldly follow your lead in truth. Lord, lead as You will. Amen.*

# Easy Like...

## Theos Pas Paraklesis[1]
## "God of All Comfort"

---

*Blessed be the God and Father of our Lord Jesus Christ, the Father of mercies and **God of all comfort**, who comforts us in all our tribulation, that we may be able to comfort those who are in any trouble, with the comfort with which we ourselves are comforted by God.*
(2 Corinthians 1:3-4, NKJV) [2]

---

It is difficult to offer comfort to others when we are in the midst of our own struggles and needing what we are wanting to give them - comfort. As many of us do, we offer prayers; realistically, probably only a fraction actually prays for others in distress while we are in distress ourselves. What makes it difficult to offer comfort is the inability to give what we do not have or are in need of ourselves – total relief. People have their own vices or ways to find relief but seemingly they never fill that void that longs for peace and sustained sincere, comfort.

It is to our benefit as believers to have a connection to the Source – Theos Pas Paraklesis. In our troubles, He gives us the lasting comfort and peace required to not only get us through but to share with others. That lasting comfort and peace fills the void to an overflow. It is the reason why many question how we are able to handle situations that would typically crush the spirits of most. However, the God of all comfort keeps us filled for properly functioning daily. His comfort eases the pain of grief, distress, and regret because He carries the burden. His comfort makes living life 'Easy like Sunday Morning' – ready to rejoice in the Lord through praise and worship. We are overcomers by His grace and we are comforted by His empowering Spirit.

## PRAYER

*Theos Pas Paraklesis! Thank You for being here at all times. There is no border of grief, distress, or regret that You are not able to break through. You are our Rescuer, with arms of compassion. It is by Your mercy we are able to receive Your comfort. You take care of Your children with tender love and kindness. No matter the depth of troubles, You hear our cry, You see our pain, You become our Comforter. All that we receive from You is in abundance and it is out of that abundance that we are able to pour into the lives of others. We are helped to be of help.*

*We comforted to comfort. We receive mercy to give mercy. Thank You for reaching all through all – glory to You. Lord, thanks for setting up chain reactions as testimonies of Your love. All blessings belong to You and with my lips and hands I offer the blessing of praise unto you. Amen.*

# SUMMARY

This book was written with the intent of illustrating prayer as essential in our daily living. The deeper we exercise our faith in prayer, the more we are apt to hear and see God at work on our behalf at all levels of life. Prayer changes our perspectives about situations that appear to be overwhelming by bringing us into the presence of the Almighty God – ensuring us of victory.

Let us wholeheartedly seek God by developing a lifestyle of prayer. It is in the prayer meeting room where we learn, receive direction, and become empowered for defeating whatever the day brings. Prayer brings us out of excuses and into results!

# NOTES

1. Biblehub (n.d.). *Names of God in the Bible*. Strong's Concordance. Retrieved from https://biblescan.com/
2. Biblical scriptures and various versions. BibleGateway. Retrieved from https://www.biblegateway.com/passage/

## Author Owen Watson, Ph.D.

Read biography and get an exclusive inside look at exciting new titles.

www.drowenwatson.com

Email: hello@authorowenwatson.com

# BOOKS BY
# Author Owen Watson, Ph.D.

What Matters Most: Family, Friends, and Foes

Po' Man Ain't Got Not Much Say

Defeating Cancer One Poem a Day

Betting on Me: Revelatory Concepts for Success

www.ingramcontent.com/pod-product-compliance
Lightning Source LLC
LaVergne TN
LVHW020541100826
845148LV00010B/1561